Michigan Trees Worth Knowing

by Norman F. Smith

Photographs by the author

published by
Thunder Bay Press
Lansing, Michigan

ABOUT THE AUTHOR . . .

Norm Smith is a native of Ann Arbor and a graduate forester, with A.B., B.S.F., and M.F. degrees from the University of Michigan, where he specialized in forest management and forest recreation.

His career with the Department of Natural Resources spanned the years from 1937 to 1976, including 27 years with the Forestry Division in Lansing during which time he was involved with forest use planning and development. He played a direct role in the growth of the State Forest campground system in the 1950s, in the establishment of scenic forest drives and riding and hiking trails, and in the preparation of informational material.

From 1964 until his retirement in 1976 he was Chief of the Office of Planning Services, responsible for the development of the state-wide Michigan Recreation Plan, and for initiating the Natural Rivers and Wilderness and Natural Areas programs. In 1966 he was appointed to the State Board of Registration for Foresters, and served as a member for ten years.

Norm is a collector of old things, and his "retirement office" in his home in East Lansing contains such collectibles as log marks from the early lumbering days and antique wooden tools. His interest in exploring the history and uses of trees and in tree photography has been both a hobby and an avocation throughout his career.

The first edition of "Michigan Trees Worth Knowing" was published in 1948 by the Conservation Department, now Department of Natural Resources. The book was enlarged in subsequent editions; and the present volume, introducing color, is a further expansion by the author, undertaken since his retirement.

Gypsy Moth Update

Since the 1978 revision of "Michigan Trees Worth Knowing" the gypsy moth has become a major problem in Michigan, particularly in the northern part of the state. It annually defoliates millions of acres in the northeastern United States. Especially susceptible are oaks, aspens, white birch, willows and basswood. Repeated defoliations may kill individual trees or whole areas.

THUNDER BAY PRESS

INTRODUCTION

O F MICHIGAN'S GREAT WEALTH OF NATURAL RESOURCES FEW have been more important in the past or are more highly valued today than our forests and the trees which make them. Not only are they a continuous source of raw materials for industry and agriculture but they affect the climate, water resources, and soil, furnish food and shelter for wildlife and are indispensable to our vast recreational and scenic areas.

Industries which depend upon trees for their existence are major employers and rank high in the State's economy. The annual production and manufacture of forest products is measured in billions of dollars. The recreation "industry," including vacation travel, resorts, food, lodging, hunting, fishing, and camping, is likewise a multi-billion dollar a year business.

It is not necessary, however, to place a monetary value on trees to appreciate them. Whether in field, fence-row, woodlot, or forest, there is an intangible wealth which they bring to millions of people through sheer enjoyment of beauty and love of nature that cannot be measured in dollars and cents. We need only to picture ourselves without trees to realize this value.

FOREST REGIONS

Michigan lies largely within the northern hardwood forest region, with areas of the central hardwood region extending up into the southern part of the state, and with pines, aspen and swamp conifers, typical of the northern coniferous forest, occupying large areas in the northern part. Due to glacial action and changes created by nature and man, lines between these broad forest classes are frequently irregular, and within each are many different types, phases, and temporary conditions, overlapping and changing with local variations of climate, soil, and moisture.

The Upper Peninsula is dominated by northern hardwood forests which occupy the better upland soils and which also occur in poorer quality on lighter soils. These stands include principally sugar maple, elm, basswood, and yellow birch, with beech present in the east half of the peninsula, and with hemlock and white pine often in mixture. The large areas of sandy plains found in many parts of the peninsula support principally pines. Spruce, balsam, cedar, and tamarack, the swamp conifers, generally occupy the poorly drained sites, while extensive areas of aspen occur throughout, principally on burned-over lands.

In the Lower Peninsula the northern hardwoods occupy the extreme northern part, extending in a broad band along the northwest side and into the central and southwestern sections. Yellow birch, hemlock, and white pine occur with less frequency or are entirely absent in these stands below the center of the state. The pines occur principally in the broad sandy plains and hills region in the north central and northeast parts. Aspen covers extensive areas of old burns throughout the north half of the Lower Peninsula, while the swamp conifers occupy the poorly drained and wet sites.

The central hardwoods, typical of states to the south, in general occupy the southern part of the Lower Peninsula and are characterized by the oaks and hickories on the dry hilly soils, by such species as sycamore, cottonwood, and silver maple on the heavier soils and bottom lands.

HISTORY

The original forest cover of Michigan has been greatly altered by agriculture, logging, and fire. When white settlement first began, 90 percent of the land area of the state was timbered. By 1840 farms were scattered over most of the southern hardwood belt and land clearing was producing more timber than was needed. Also, it was hardwood timber and not easily worked with the hand tools of the day. Much of it was burned to get rid of it.

The flood of pioneers coming to Michigan and the Midwest needed white pine for construction. Michigan had it in quantities believed to be inexhaustible. Its harvest was inevitable, and Michigan became the leading lumber-producing state in the Nation, a position held for a quarter of a century prior to 1900. This was the great, and now legendary, lumbering era, an important period in our history, and one filled with romance and glory, as well as tragedy. The wealth produced in this period was largely responsible for the great financial and industrial rise of the state.

Once under way logging progressed rapidly, and by 1900 most of the pine in the Lower Peninsula was gone. Pine logging in the Upper Peninsula began to assume importance in the 1880's and the virgin stands lasted until about 1920. The peak of Michigan's great timber harvest was reached in 1890 when mills cut a total of 5.5 billion board feet of lumber, mostly pine. This is more than 5 times our present annual production of all species. White and red pine, once the backbone of the industry, now make up less than five percent of the cut.

There had been little demand for hardwood timber until the end of the pine was in sight. Hardwood lumbering in the north part of the Lower Peninsula occupied the period from 1890 to 1920, and progressed through virgin stands in the Upper Peninsula from about 1910 to 1940, when almost no virgin timber stands remained outside of reserved areas. The Upper Peninsula now produces over half of the total timber harvested in the state.

Forest fires were a part of the logging scene in Michigan although not necessarily the result of it. Nor were forest fires new to the state at the time logging began. Extensive burned-over areas were reported by early surveyors long before the lumbermen arrived. But the great influx of people during the logging era, and the large areas of dry pine slash increased both the possibility of fire and the intensity of those which occurred. Many reached tremendous proportion, burning unchecked for weeks or months through slashings, standing timber, cities and settlements, causing human misery, death, and waste. There is evidence to show that these lumbering era fires destroyed more merchantable timber than was cut. Most of the pine areas in the north part of the Lower Peninsula have burned over at least once, and many several times. Fires were not confined to pine lands, for hardwood slashings also burned. Large parts of these once charred lands are now occupied by jack pine, oak, aspen, and white birch, species which make up much of the second-growth forests found in northern Michigan.

OWNERSHIP OF THE RESOURCE

Of Michigan's total land area of 36 million acres, over 19 million acres are today classed as forest and wild land, nearly one-third of which is in public ownership, mostly in state and national forests, wildlife areas and parks, with state ownership comprising 4.2 million acres, and federal ownership 2.8 million. School, community, and county forests, though usually small in size and chiefly valuable for educational and recreational purposes, are part of the vast public ownership. Although public forests contain some areas of old-growth timber, they are made up largely of what were once cut-over, burned-over lands and abandoned farms, now in various stages of restocking with second-growth stands. They provide an important "multiple-use" reservoir of growing trees which is being managed for present and future timber crops, for wildlife production, public hunting, camping, wilderness enjoyment, scientific study, and many other forms of recreation and use.

The two-thirds of the forest land in private ownership is made up of nearly four million acres in farm woodlots and nine million acres in industrial and other holdings. These forests contain two-thirds of Michigan's merchantable timber volume, and presently produce three-fourths of our sawlogs for lumber and veneer, and about half of our pulpwood and other products.

FOREST PRODUCTS

Sawlog production varies between 300 and 500 million board feet annually, about equally divided between the two peninsulas. Farm woodlots in southern Michigan produce nearly 25 percent of the total cut of sawlogs, and are an extremely important source of hardwood timber due to their proximity to industrial markets and their value for local farm use. Hardwoods comprise about 85 percent of the total sawlog production in the state, and softwoods 15 percent. Michigan, once the leading lumber producer, now ranks about twentieth among the states.

Lumber, and the hundreds of items made from it, is no longer the major product of our forests in terms of wood volume, and, in fact, constitutes only about one-third of the total timber harvested. Pulpwood for paper and pressed-board products has been steadily increasing in importance, and now constitutes more than one-half of our wood output. Fuelwood comprises approximately 10 percent, and the balance is made up principally of veneer logs, excelsior bolts, mine timbers, ties, cabin logs, posts, poles, and piling.

While not actually "forest products," game and recreation associated with the forests have made Michigan's wild lands a playground of nationwide importance. The combination of trees and water found along the shores of the Great Lakes and on the inland lakes and streams annually attracts millions of tourists and resorters, hunters, fishermen, hikers and skiers. The servicing of recreational needs is the life blood of many northern Michigan communities which, after years of mere existence following the lumbering period, have come back to thrive and grow with the tourists and the second growth.

A relative newcomer in terms of forest products is the plantation-grown Christmas tree industry which has become a multi-million dollar business in Michigan, the nation's leading producer. Lesser products of the forest, but of importance either for income, home use, or for pure recreation, are maple syrup, blueberries, nuts, mushrooms, and herbs. Trees are also the sources of a variety of medicinals, flavorings, and dyes, many of which were known to the Indians and passed on by them to the early settlers, and are still in limited use today.

PROTECTION AND MANAGEMENT

The protection of our forest assets is a matter of prime importance if they are to be perpetuated. Protection from fires is, of cousre, the most important, particularly in the northern part of the state where dry, inflammable material and large, unbroken blocks of timber make even the smallest fire a real menace. Modern fire protection together with public help and understanding, however, are insurance against a repetition of the holocausts of 75 and 100 years ago.

While fires have historically been the worst enemy of trees and forests, other agents are much more destructive today. Insects and diseases, working quietly but steadily, are always present in timber stands and often on isolated forest and shade trees. Although they may only retard growth or make trees temporarily unsightly, they frequently deform, weaken, or kill. Direct control measures, such as spraying, are costly and frequently impractical unless the trees or forests being protected are of high value. Under forest conditions the most practical means of preventing serious outbreaks is through management to produce healthy stands. This is accomplished through elimination of diseased or defective trees, by encouraging mixtures of species, thereby reducing the concentration of host trees available to a specific insect or disease, and by other cultural practices such as pruning, manipulation of stocking, and eradication of alternate hosts.

Poor and unwise cutting practices are another menace to our timber resource. Destructive methods which remove trees as soon as they reach merchantable size or which make no provision for regeneration of the stand, are still used on many private lands but becoming less common. Grazing of farm woodlots is a harmful practice which destroys young seedlings and damages older trees through injury to the roots and compacting of the soil. Similarly, in many northern localities where deer have become too numerous for their normal food supplies, continuous and heavy browsing of forest reproduction is detrimental to both the forest and the deer herd.

Trees are a renewable resource, and, unless the land is converted to some other permanent use, will replace themselves in time in spite of cutting, fire, insects, disease, and the extremes of weather. We may be willing to wait for the slow and often uncertain processes of unaided nature, or we may speed them up and control them by the application of appropriate management practices.

Management of this resource may take different directions depending upon the objectives—timber crops, wildlife production, landscape enhancement, recreation, preservation, or protection of aesthetic values. Public foresters and land managers apply modern techniques and laws to reach these objectives and to assure the continuous supply of a wide variety of products and services. Large industrial forest owners, and more and more small owners, employ professional foresters to carry out forest management which will assure sustained production of tree crops and protection of other values. The services of public forestry agencies are available for advice and assistance to private forest owners on management problems.

Trees interest people for different reasons. Regardless of the basis of interest, a knowledge of our common trees, their characteristics and uses, will lead to a fuller enjoyment of the out-of-doors and a deeper appreciation of their value in our lives.

TABLE OF CONTENTS

TREE NAME	Page
Ailanthus—*Ailanthus altissima* (Mill.) Swingle	84
Ash, Black—*Fraxinus nigra* Marsh.	81
Ash, White—*Fraxinus americana* L.	80
Aspen, Largetooth—*Populus grandidentata*, Michx.	21
Aspen, Quaking—*Populus tremuloides* Michx.	20
Balm-of-Gilead—*Populus balsamifera* L.	22
Basswood—*Tilia americana* L.	79
Beech—*Fagus grandifolia* Ehrh.	34
Beech, Blue—*Carpinus caroliniana* Walt.	35
Birch, White—*Betula papyrifera* Marsh.	31
Birch, Yellow—*Betula alleghaniensis* Michx. f.	30
Box Elder—*Acer negundo* L.	77
Butternut—*Juglans cinerea* L.	25
Catalpa, Northern—*Catalpa speciosa* Warder	85
Cedar, Red—*Juniperus virginiana* L.	18
Cedar, White, or Arborvitae—*Thuja occidentalis* L.	17
Cherry, Black—*Prunus serotina* Ehrh.	68
Cherry, Choke—*Prunus virginiana* L.	43
Cherry, Pin—*Prunus pensylvanica* L.f.	42
Chestnut, American—*Castanea dentata* (Marsh.) Borkh.	55
Cottonwood—*Populus deltoides* Marsh.	23
Crab, Wild—*Malus coronaria* (L.) Mill.	40
Dogwood, Flowering—*Cornus florida* L.	49
Elm, American—*Ulmus americana* L.	63
Elm, Rock—*Ulmus thomasii* Sarg.	65
Elm, Slippery—*Ulmus fulva* Michx.	64
Fir, Balsam—*Abies balsamea* (L.) Mill.	16
Ginkgo—*Ginkgo biloba* L.	83
Gum, Black—*Nyssa sylvatica* Marsh.	82
Hackberry—*Celtis occidentalis* L.	66
Hawthorn—*Crataegus* species L.	44
Hemlock—*Tsuga canadensis* (L.) Carr.	15
Hickories, Pignut—*Carya glabra* (Mill.) Sweet	27
Carya ovalis (Wang.) Sarg.	27
Hickory, Bitternut—*Carya cordiformis* (Wang.) K.Koch	28
Hickory, Shagbark—*Carya ovata* (Mill.) K.Koch	26
Honeylocust—*Gleditsia triacanthos* L.	70
Horsechestnut—*Aesculus hippocastanum* L.	78
Ironwood—*Ostrya virginiana* (Mill.) K.Koch	29
Juneberry—*Amelanchier laevis* Wieg.	39
Kentucky Coffee-tree—*Gymnocladus dioica* (L.) K.Koch	69
Locust, Black—*Robinia pseudoacacia* L.	71
Maple, Black—*Acer nigrum* Michx. f.	73
Maple, Mountain—*Acer spicatum* Lam.	46
Maple, Norway—*Acer plantanoides* L.	76
Maple, Red—*Acer rubrum* L.	74
Maple, Silver—*Acer saccharinum* L.	75
Maple, Striped—*Acer pensylvanicum* L.	47
Maple, Sugar—*Acer saccharum* Marsh.	72
Mountain Ash—*Sorbus* species L.	38
Mulberry—*Morus* species L.	36
Nannyberry—*Viburnum lentago* L.	48
Oak, Black—*Quercus velutina* Lamarck	61
Oak, Bur—*Quercus macrocarpa* Michx.	57
Oak, Chinquapin—*Quercus muehlenbergii* Engelm.	59
Oak, Northern Red—*Quercus rubra* L.	60
Oak, Pin—*Quercus palustris* Muenchh.	62
Oak, Swamp White—*Quercus bicolor* Willd.	58
Oak, White—*Quercus alba* L.	56
Paw Paw—*Asimina triloba* (L.) Dunal	37
Pine, Austrian—*Pinus nigra* Arnold	10
Pine, Jack—*Pinus banksiana* Lamb.	8
Pine, Red or Norway—*Pinus resinosa* Ait.	7
Pine, Scotch—*Pinus sylvestris* L.	9
Pine, White—*Pinus strobus* L.	6
Plum, Canada—*Prunus nigra* Ait.	41
Plum, Wild—*Prunus americana* Marsh.	41
Redbud—*Cercis canadensis* L.	45
Sassafras—*Sassafras albidum* (Nutt.) Nees	32
Spruce, Black—*Picea mariana* (Mill.) B.S.P.	13
Spruce, Norway—*Picea abies* (L.) Karst.	14
Spruce, White—*Picea glauca* (Moench.) Voss	12
Sycamore—*Platanus occidentalis* L.	33
Tamarack—*Larix laricina* (Du Roi) K.Koch	11
Tulip Poplar—*Liriodendron tulipifera* L.	67
Walnut, Black—*Juglans nigra* L.	24
Willow, Black—*Salix nigra* Marsh.	19

	Page
About Tree Flowers and Winter Buds	50
Forest Succession—A Northern Michigan Case History	51-53
Glossary	87
Leaf Terminology	86
References	Inside Back Cover
Scientific Tree Nomenclature	Inside Back Cover
Small Trees	35
When Autumn Comes	54
Wood to Burn	88

The trees described herein are, for the most part, also found in Wisconsin, Minnesota, and neighboring Ontario.

WHITE PINE

Pinus strobus L.

WHITE PINE WAS AT ONE TIME THE backbone of the lumber industry in Michigan and the Lake States. From 1870 to 1890, Michigan led the nation in lumber production. Here were the greatest stands of white pine the world had ever seen, and here also was an enormous demand for cheap building material for the rapidly expanding Midwest. The lumbermen answered this call, and the industry which developed and flourished was a primary factor in the great financial, industrial and commercial rise of Michigan. In recognition of its beauty and contribution, white pine has been designated as the official state tree of Michigan.

The natural occurrence of white pine in the state is principally in the Upper Peninsula and the north half of the Lower Peninsula, although it occurs as far south as Allegan, Eaton and St. Clair counties and can be successfully planted even in the most southern counties. Some of the best stands in the state once grew in the vicinity of Alma and Mt. Pleasant, and white pine stump fences still found in this locality are reminders of that timber. White pine figures prominently in the public and private reforestation activities of Michigan.

White pine grows in nearly pure stands, or mixed with red (Norway) pine, or with hardwoods and hemlock. It is best adapted to moist sandy loam soils but will grow on a variety of sites from swamp to dry sand. It prefers the shade of other trees when young, being easily injured by drying winds and intense heat. At first slow growing, it later grows from one foot to two and one-half feet or sometimes more in height in one year, finally attaining a height of 80 to 120 feet at maturity with a diameter of from three to four feet. Trees 150 to 200 feet tall with diameters of five to seven feet were occasionally reported by the early loggers. Under forest conditions the mature trees have narrow irregular crowns, but when grown in the open, the crown is symmetrical and broad. Tops of tall exposed white pines are often bent away from the direction of the prevailing winds and flattened on the windward side.

The bark of white pine is smooth, dark greenish brown on young trees, gray and deeply grooved on older trees. The needles occur in clusters of five, and this is the only five-needle pine native to the eastern United States. The needles are three to five inches long, pale blue green in color, and are fine and soft.

The flowers of white pine occur as small cones in May and June, the staminate or male flowers on the lower branches and the ovulate or female cone-producing flowers on the upper branches. The drooping cones are four to eight inches long, narrow and tapering, with rather loose flexible scales, opening in September of the second year. The seeds are brown, about ¼-inch long and average about 25,000 per pound. They are a preferred food of red squirrels which often cache the green cones in large piles for the winter. The winter buds are slender and sharp pointed, about ¼-to ½-inch long.

Branching along the main stem occurs nearly at right angles to it, in a whorl-like arrangement, a new whorl being formed with each year's growth. The ages of young trees can be closely determined by counting these whorls of branches or branch scars.

The white pine weevil and the white pine blister rust are the two main enemies of this pine in Michigan. The weevil attacks and kills the terminal shoots causing the trees to become deformed and crooked. Blister rust, which attacks all five-needle pines, is caused by a fungus which slowly girdles the branches and main stem. The fungus requires the presence of gooseberry or currant bushes on which to complete its life cycle. Spores are blown from bushes to tree needles where infection takes place. At a certain period tree-produced spores return to the bushes to develop this stage of growth.

Two-thirds of the white pine timber volume is in the Upper Peninsula, largely in the western part, where the largest volume exists as old-growth trees mixed in the hardwood forests. In the Lower Peninsula two small remaining stands of virgin pine are preserved in the Interlochen and Hartwick Pines State Parks. The annual cut of white pine is less than five percent of the total board foot production in the state, and in sharp contrast to the white pine cut in 1889, when it represented 65 percent of the total timber cut in the state that year. Cutting of white pine today is carried on along with other timber operations for the pine occurs in widely scattered patches or as single trees in mixture with other species.

White pine wood is creamy-white to reddish brown, soft, straight-grained and uniform in texture. It is easily worked and nails exceptionally well. A cubic foot of seasoned wood weighs 25 pounds. The principal white pine products in Michigan are lumber, sash, millwork, paneling, interior finish, and boxes. It is a favorite wood for hand-carved duck decoys.

Identifying characteristics: Needles, five in a cluster, three to five inches long, blue green, soft; cones, long, tapering, with flexible scales; branches, whorl-like, extending nearly at right angles to main stem; bark, smooth, greenish brown on young trees, gray, deeply grooved on older trees.

RED OR NORWAY PINE

Pinus resinosa Ait.

CLOSELY ASSOCIATED WITH WHITE PINE is one of Michigan's most picturesque trees, the stately red or Norway pine. Occasionally reaching a height of 125 feet or more, its slender, columnar trunk may rise more than two-thirds of its height free from branches. Old survivors of logging and fires are familiar sights, breaking the skyline of northern Michigan landscapes. Never as plentiful as white pine, nor valued as highly, it nevertheless formed an important part of the virgin stands, amounting to an estimated 15 percent of the original pine timber cut. Today the proportion of red pine to white pine is considerably greater, and its value as a timber species and in reforestation make it one of the state's most important trees.

The name "Norway" pine is misleading, as the tree is native to this country and does not occur naturally in Norway at all. It has been claimed both that it received this name from the town of Norway, Maine, where it was at one time abundant; and that an early explorer confused it with the Scotch pine of Norway, due to the similarity in color of bark. The name "red" pine, however, is descriptive as the bark is distinctly reddish in color.

Intermediate between white and jack pine in its soil preference, red pine grows well in mixture with white pine on heavy loam soils and with jack pine on the lighter sandy soils. Best growth, however, is attained on well-drained sands, sandy loams and gravels. Due to the broad range of soils on which it will grow, its generally rapid growth, and the high value of its timber yield, red pine is more extensively planted today in Michigan than any other species. Easy to establish, it frequently grows one to two feet in height a year. It can be planted with success in any part of the state and is increasing in importance as a Christmas tree.

The trunks of forest-grown trees taper slowly, rising straight from the ground into broad, dome-shaped, rather open, slightly pointed crowns. Heights of mature trees range usually from 60 to 100 feet with diameters of two to three feet. The lower branches die out rapidly under shaded forest conditions, giving the trees the characteristic long, clear boles. Open-grown trees have broad, rounded crowns reaching to the ground when young, the lower branches persisting for many years. Branching as in white pine, occurs in whorls around the main stem, extending nearly at right angles to it. A new whorl is formed each year.

At first thin and papery, the reddish-brown bark later becomes thick, shallowly grooved, and divided into broad, flaky plates. The heavy bark is fire-resistant, protecting old trees through fires which may completely destroy surrounding small timber and brush.

Needles of the red pine are four to six inches long, the longest of the three native Michigan pines. Dark green, lustrous and sharp pointed, they occur in pairs held together at one end by a sheath, and remain on the branches for four to five years. They break readily when doubled. The foliage occurs in tufts, markedly different in appearance from the plume-like foliage of the white pine or the ragged foliage of the jack pine. The winter buds are about ¾-inch long and sharp pointed.

Clusters of dark purple staminate flowers about ½-inch long occur in May and June on the lower branches of the tree, while on the upper branches the less conspicuous scarlet ovulate flowers occur. The cones mature by autumn of the second season, a good seed year occurring only once in four to seven years. Mature cones are egg-shaped, about two inches long, light brown, with firm scales. The seeds are light brown, winged, ½- to ¾-inch long, and about 50,000 weigh one pound.

Red pine has few serious diseases, but destructive insect pests have multiplied with the establishment of large areas of plantations. Most destructive are the root collar weevils which girdle young trees at the ground level; the spittlebugs which suck juices from the needles, turning them brown and reducing their vigor by killing twigs and branches; and the red-headed pine sawflys whose larvae devour the needles, killing the trees after repeated attacks. Less serious is the European pine shoot moth which attacks the terminal growth.

The present merchantable volumes of natural red pine in Michigan occur largely in second growth stands or as scattered old-growth trees in restocking and deforested areas. About half occurs in the north half of the Lower Peninsula, half in the Upper Peninsula. Red pine plantations are increasingly important as a source of wood.

The wood of the red pine is reddish and stiff. It is slightly heavier, harder and more resinous than white pine. It is classed with the so-called "hard pines" found in the southern states. In Michigan it is used chiefly in construction, millwork, piling, utility poles, barn poles, cabin logs, highway guardrail posts, mine timbers and pulpwood. The lumber is often mixed with white pine and sold commercially as "white pine." A cubic foot of seasoned wood weighs 34 pounds. Red pine stumps and roots are very pitchy and make excellent kindling for fires.

Identifying characteristics: Needles in pairs, four to six inches long, sheathed, break readily when doubled; foliage with tufted appearance; cones egg-shaped, small; bark red-brown, papery on young trees, flaky on older trees; trunks of old trees columnar.

7

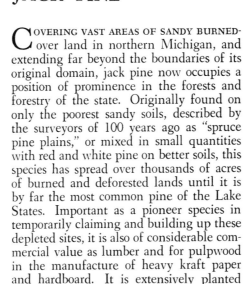

JACK PINE

Pinus banksiana Lamb.

COVERING VAST AREAS OF SANDY BURNED-over land in northern Michigan, and extending far beyond the boundaries of its original domain, jack pine now occupies a position of prominence in the forests and forestry of the state. Originally found on only the poorest sandy soils, described by the surveyors of 100 years ago as "spruce pine plains," or mixed in small quantities with red and white pine on better soils, this species has spread over thousands of acres of burned and deforested lands until it is by far the most common pine of the Lake States. Important as a pioneer species in temporarily claiming and building up these depleted sites, it is also of considerable commercial value as lumber and for pulpwood in the manufacture of heavy kraft paper and hardboard. It is extensively planted on dry sites less favorable to other species.

The importance of this species to the survival of the rare Kirtland's warbler is now well established. A special management unit in Crawford, Oscoda and Ogemaw counties is dedicated to providing a continuous succession of areas with 10 to 15 foot jack pines, the required habitat of this bird.

Jack pine is definitely a northern Michigan tree, seldom occurring naturally south of Grand Haven and Saginaw. Northward, its range extends far into Canada. Ordinarily it occupies the light, dry, sandy soils, but it may be found on heavier soils, and even in wet bogs with black spruce and tamarack. A prolific seeder following fires, it frequently comes up in extremely dense stands. However, competition for light soon forces large numbers to die out. Stands of this type produce tall spindly trees with small crowns and slender stems. Many such stands become stagnated, the individual trees growing very slowly. Besides occurring in pure stands, jack pine is also found in mixtures with oak, aspen, spruce, balsam, white birch and the other pines.

Under ordinary conditions, jack pine matures in about 60 years, reaching heights of 50 to 60 feet with diameters of 10 to 15 inches. Stands containing trees 18 to 20 inches or more in diameter with heights of over 70 feet are occasionally found near Lake Superior. Open-grown jack pines occasionally reach these diameters but are much shorter, with broad, irregular, open crowns. The lower branches of this species die out rapidly when shaded but remain on the tree for many years, giving it a ragged appearance unlike white or red pine. Height growth on young trees may well exceed two feet a year slowing up considerably toward middle age. Branching is irregular, two or three whorls being formed every year.

On new growth and young trees the bark is light brown in color and only slightly scaly, becoming dark brown and finally dark gray or black, with loose scales on the older branches and irregular, scaly ridges on the trunk. Except on young seedlings, where they frequently exceed three inches in length, the needles are ¾- to 1½-inches long, stout, dark yellow-green. They occur in spreading pairs held together at the base by a short sheath, and remain on the branches from two to three years. Clustered yellow staminate flowers occur in May and June, shedding clouds of yellow pollen when shaken. The ovulate flowers are purplish. The cones are 1½- to 2-inches long, light greenish brown, tough, and frequently quite crooked. They are formed annually but require two years to mature. They occur singly or in twos or threes and are frequently borne on young trees only five or six years old. Not stalked, they hold firmly to the branches and may remain 20 years or more unopened, thus conserving the seed to reproduce the trees in large quantities when the heat of a fire finally opens them. The black seeds, including the wing, are about 1/3-inch long. Approximately 150,000 cleaned seeds are required to make a pound.

The terminal winter bud is nearly ¼-inch long, light brown in color, and rounded. The lateral buds are smaller.

Jack pine has its share of insects and diseases. Most serious are the pack pine sawfly and jack pine budworm, both of which feed on the needles and are capable of defoliating and ultimately killing whole stands with repeated attacks. Normally less serious are the spittlebug, white pine weevil, and anomala beetle. A disease causing "red-heart" does considerable damage in old stands and causes "dozy" or soft lumber.

Forests in which jack pine predominates occupy over one million acres in Michigan. Sixty percent of this area is located in the north half of the Lower Peninsula, particularly in the central part of this region. Very little old-growth timber is left, most of the volume occurring in second-growth and reforested areas.

Jack pine wood is light, soft, close grained, and not very strong. The sapwood is thick, nearly white. A cubic foot of air-dryed jack pine wood weighs 30 pounds. Its principal uses in Michigan are for lumber, pulpwood, mine timbers, fish boxes, pallets, and round-faced vertical cabin siding. For interior paneling it is very knotty and colorful.

Identifying characteristics: Needles in pairs, about one inch long; young bark tan, old bark dark gray, scaly; cones and dead branches persisting for many years; cones small, crooked.

SCOTCH PINE

Pinus sylvestris L.

SCOTCH PINE IS A NATIVE OF NORTHERN Europe where it is more properly called "Scots" pine. It is the only conifer truly native to the British Isles. It is one of the most important timber trees in Europe where natural stands and plantations are managed for production of lumber, pulpwood, turpentine and resin. Several races or varieties are known, each adapted to its particular location.

It is not known when Scotch pine was first brought to America, but it was planted in colonial times in New England and elsewhere as an ornamental, later for reforestation, windbreaks and shelterbelts, and most recently for the production of Christmas trees. It has become naturalized in many areas. Use of this species in reforestation began toward the end of the last century in the vanguard of the conservation movement. The foresters of that period were European trained, and Scotch pine and other European trees were more familiar to them than were the native American species.

In Michigan, with thousands of acres of northern cut-over and burned-over lands and abondoned farms in need of restocking, Scotch pine was one of the earliest to be experimented with, as early as 1888. It figured in Michigan's reforestation program until 1920 when, because of its crooked trunks and limbiness, largely reflections of site and insect attacks, it was abondoned in favor of native species which were more suited to light, sandy, depleted soils, grew straighter and equally as fast. Many of these early plantations are still growing in the state forests and other areas, principally in the northern Lower Peninsula. Small plantings are commonly seen throughout the state, and individual trees are favorites in parks, cemeteries and homesites. Some of the largest are found in the front yards of farm homes where they were planted in the early part of this century with Austrian pine and Norway spruce, two other imports from Europe.

Scotch pine has returned to prominence in recent years for a purpose not dreamed of by its early promoters—Christmas trees. Since the early fifties this industry has grown into a multi-million dollar business, with Christmas tree plantations occupying thousands of acres of private land formerly in agriculture or timber production, mainly in the Lower Peninsula. This species makes up about 85 percent of the Christmas trees marketed in Michigan; and it is the basis for a large export business which sends Michigan-grown trees as far away as Texas and Florida. Quality trees do not "just grow." They are the result of research in genetics and seed selection, careful planting, cultivating and spraying for insects and disease, and of several shearings during the 6 to 10 years of growth to form the compact, pyramidal shape sought by purchasers.

As open-grown landscape trees, Scotch pine may grow to 50 to 70 feet in height, developing a wide, round topped, irregular crown, and a trunk one to two feet in diameter. In old plantations the crowns are slender and pointed, much like other pines. Branches are persistent along the trunks, and trunks may be distorted as a result of genetic characteristics, site deficiencies, or early insect attacks.

The characteristic orange color of the bark on the upper trunk and branches provides quick identification of Scotch pine. On these parts of the tree the bark is thin, smooth and flaky. On old trunks it becomes dark orange-brown, thick, and deeply grooved. Needles are two in a cluster, sheathed at the base, 1½ to 3 inches long, stiff, sharp pointed, and more or less twisted. They are normally blue-green or gray-green, although various strains range from yellow-green to steel-blue.

Flowers appear in May and June, both sexes on the same tree. They are about ¼ inch long and occur in clusters, the reddish female ovules in the upper part of the tree, the pollen bearing male flowers in the lower part. The cones mature in autumn of the second season, hanging in clusters of two or three. They are egg-shaped, usually symmetrical, about 1½ to 2½ inches long, with tan to gray-brown scales terminating in a minute prickle. The winged seeds are red-brown in color, about ¼ inch long, and number about 75,000 to the pound. Winter buds are about ¼ inch long, pointed, reddish brown and resinous.

Scotch pine is attacked by a variety of insects which damage or destroy needles, shoots and trunks. Among these are the Zimmerman pine moth, European pine sawfly, Pales weevil, and pine root collar weevil. Buds are often fed on by the pine grosbeak causing distortion and lack of branching, both serious to Christmas tree growers.

The wood is red-brown in color with thick yellow or pinkish sapwood. It is light in weight, straight grained, hard and resinous. These properties would lend it to the same uses as red and jack pines, but its supply is too limited to figure in commercial production in this country.

Identifying characteristics: Needles in pairs, 1½ to 3 inches long, stiff and sharp, often with bluish cast; cones egg-shaped, symmetrical, with minute prickles on scales; bark on branches and upper trunk orange and flaky.

AUSTRIAN PINE

Pinus nigra Arnold

Austrian pine ranks with Scotch pine as one of Europe's important forest and timber trees. It is a native of the mountainous regions of southern Europe and Asia Minor where several geographic varieties are recognized; and it has been extensively planted on the Continent for its products of lumber, pulp and turpentine, and as an ornamental and soil stabilizer. Its tolerance of salt spray has led to its use in dune and erosion control in the maritime areas bordering the Mediterranean. It has been cultivated in America for more than 200 years.

Although this species is most commonly called Austrian pine in this country, in Europe it is known as "black pine," as its botanical name implies. Its most common varieties are Austrian and Corsican pines, named for their geographic origins. The Austrian variety was introduced into America in 1759, and found early acceptance as an ornamental and for windbreaks. Over the years it has been widely used in city parks, cemeteries, and residential landscaping. It is one of the large, picturesque evergreens often seen in farmyards where it was planted in the early part of this century along with Scotch pine and Norway spruce.

Its dense form, rapid growth, and ability to flourish under harsh climatic conditions and on a variety of soils led to the extensive use of Austrian pine in the dust-bowl Shelterbelt Project of the 1930s. It was the first species planted at the project dedication ceremonies in Oklahoma in 1935, launching this ambitious soil conservation program which extended in a band 100 miles wide from North Dakota to Texas, and which by 1942 had used 217 million trees and shrubs on more than 18,000 miles of shelterbelts across six states.

In recent years Austrian pine has been planted in small quantities for Christmas trees; and it has found increasing use in highway landscaping in southern Michigan because if its pleasing form, its tolerance of adverse sites and conditions, and especially its resistance to salt injury.

Austrian pine is a rugged looking, heavy-crowned tree in all stages of development. Young trees have a dense, conical shape which becomes more open, and rounded or flat-topped at maturity. In general outline it resembles our native red pine, but it has a more massive bearing. It grows to heights of 60 to 100 feet and diameters of two to three feet, with a straight trunk and slightly downswept branches which radiate in spoke-like whorls. Young trees retain their lower branches longer than most pines, a fact which adds to the value of Austrian pine for screening, windbreaks and wildlife shelter.

The bark of Austrian pine is composed of scaly plates separated by vertical grooves.

It is gray-brown to almost black, flaking off on old exposed trunks to produce a surface mottled with grays and browns. The twigs are tan and roughened by old needle bases. Winter buds are reddish brown or silvery, resinous, about ½ inch long, dome-shaped and pointed.

The needles are dark green, the darkest of the pines found in Michigan. In clusters of two, they are four to seven inches long, stiff and sharp pointed, with a flat inner side. The edges are roughened by very fine teeth. The needle pairs are held by a short black sheath, and they persist on the branches for four to six years. When bent double, the needles do not break cleanly as red pine needles do.

The flowers appear in May or June, the male or pollen-bearing in yellow, cylindrical clusters, ¾ inch long, at the base of the young shoots; the female in smaller, bright red, cone-like clusters at the tips of the new growth. The cones appear singly or in clusters of two or three, maturing in the autumn of the second year. They are two to four inches long, narrowly pyramidal when closed, and broadly dome-shaped when open. They are tan to gray-brown and somewhat shiny, with a sharp spur or prickle on the thickened scale. The seeds are reddish brown, ¼ inch long, with wings about ¾ inch long. There is an average of about 26,000 seeds per pound.

While considered relatively free from serious insects and diseases when growing singly or in small open plantings along highways, under more crowded conditions Austrian pine may be attacked by several pests. The shoots are susceptible to damage by the Zimmerman pine moth and European pine shootmoth. The European pine sawfly may be destructive to the needles. New shoots may also be killed by a tip blight disease. Seed source plays an important role in resistance to these attacks, and seed from Yugoslavia is now considered the best. One other frequent pest is the yellow-bellied sapsucker which drills holes through the bark, often in neat rows. These penetrations may provide avenues for disease organisms to enter the trunk.

The wood of Austrian pine is soft, light in weight, and very resinous. It is reddish brown with thick yellow to pink sapwood. It is not used commercially in this country.

Identifying characteristics: Needles in pairs, four to seven inches long, dark green, do not break readily when doubled; foliage dense; cones two to four inches long with sharp spurs on scales; bark flaky, brown-gray to black, or mottled with gray on old exposed trunks.

TAMARACK

Larix laricina (Du Roi) K. Koch

Tamarack, known to many as larch, is distinct among the conifers in that it sheds its needles annually in the fall of each year when the hardwoods drop their leaves. Three species of the genus *Larix* are native to North America: western larch, an important timber tree; alpine larch, a relatively unimportant, high-altitude, western tree; and eastern larch, or tamarack, found abundantly in the three Lake States of Wisconsin, Minnesota and Michigan, and northward into Canada. Several exotic species and varieties are planted in the United States as ornamentals, and have been used in reforestation to a limited extent.

In southern Michigan, where tamarack is approaching the southern limt of its range, occurrence of this tree is confined almost entirely to small pure stands in cold bogs and sphagnum swamps. In the northern part of the state tamarack occurs in swamps frequently in mixture with black spruce, and also on the better drained upland soils where it is associated with balsam, white birch and aspen. Exceedingly intolerant of shade, it is usually a dominant tree where it occurs under forest conditions.

Ordinarily tamarack does not develop into a very large tree, 50 to 75 feet high and one to two feet in diameter being the usual ranges of mature trees, although trees 100 feet tall and two and one-half feet in diameter have been found. Ages of over 200 years are not uncommon in old stands.

Tamaracks grown under crowded forest conditions have narrow, open, pyramidal crowns and short horizontal branches, while open-grown trees have denser foliage and sweeping, gracefully curved branches. Growth is fairly rapid during the early life of the tree, slowing up considerably after 40 or 50 years, especially on extremely wet soils. The root system of tamarack is shallow and spreading, and on drier soils easily damaged by surface fires.

The bark on young branches is smooth, at first grayish, becoming light orange-brown. On the older branches it is dark gray, while on the trunks of old trees it is light reddish brown and scaly.

The soft flexible needles of tamarack are light blue-green in color, triangular in cross section, and from ¾- to 1¼-inches long. On the new growth they occur singly and are arranged alternately along the twigs, while on the older stems they occur in spreading clusters of 10 or more on short spurs. In the fall of each year the needles turn straw-yellow or buff color and drop off. This autumn change in color and loss of needles is alarming to many persons, not acquainted with this species, who think the trees are dying or are dead.

In the spring along with the needles the small flowers appear—the staminate flowers yellow and nearly round, the ovulate oblong with green-tipped bracts and conspicuous rose-red scales. The small, upright oval cones occur the following autumn on short incurved stalks. They are made up of about 20 light brown, thin scales. Seeds are shed during the fall and winter, but the open cones persist for a year or more. The seeds are about ⅛-inch long, triangular, with a chestnut-brown wing. Cleaned seeds will number 100,000 to 150,000 to the pound.

Most serious enemy of tamarack is the leaf-eating larva of the larch sawfly which was apparently introduced from Europe about 1853, when it was first noticed in the vicinity of Quebec. After doing enormous damage in the East, particularly in Maine, it became established in Michigan about 1897 and in Minnesota about 1910. Millions of tamaracks were killed in the ensuing years, and today almost no old-growth trees are left in the Lake States. Dead poles resulting from these attacks remain standing even today. This pest still causes periodic trouble in second growth stands. Damage to tamarack by disease, while always present in stands to some degree, is relatively unimportant in Michigan.

Approximately 40 percent of the tamarack area is in the eastern half of the Upper Peninsula, and 15 percent in the south half of the Lower Peninsula. The annual cut of tamarack for lumber is small, but considerable quantities of ties, mine props and fuel wood are produced.

Tamarack wood is hard, strong, and durable in contact with the soil. The heaviest of Michigan's softwoods, it weighs 37 pounds per cubic foot when seasoned. It is light brown in color with pronounced growth rings, the line between the light colored spring-wood and the dark colored summer-wood being very distinct. The wood is used principally for posts, poles, pulp, mine timbers, ties, boxes, crates, lumber and mill-work.

Identifying characteristics: Needles light blue-green, soft, in clusters on short spurs, needles deciduous, spurs remaining; young twigs light orange-brown, smooth; old trunks reddish brown, scaly; generally found in swamps and on low moist ground.

WHITE SPRUCE

Picea glauca (Moench.) Voss

Most beautiful of the eastern spruces, white spruce is important among the native trees of Michigan for its commercial value as pulpwood and saw timber, and because it is grown in large numbers for landscaping and reforestation.

Found in the extreme north part of the Lower Peninsula and throughout the Upper Peninsula, this spruce occurs occasionally in small pure stands but more often is mixed with other species. It is a common tree of lake shores, stream borders and moist uplands. Its best growth is attained on sandy-loam soils on which it may grow in association with white pine, hard maple, yellow birch or aspen. Or it may be found on low, wet ground along with black spruce, balsam fir, tamarack, balm-of-Gilead and red maple. It is tolerant of shade, but not as tolerant as black spruce.

Straight stemmed and narrow crowned, forest-grown white spruces reach heights of 70 feet or more at maturity, and have diameters up to two feet, with larger sizes found occasionally. The tips of the trees usually are not as pointed as those of the black spruce, and may be quite rounded or blunt. The branches prune themselves well under shaded conditions, so the trunk may be clear for from one-third to two-thirds of the height of the tree. Open-grown trees have broader and more symmetrical crowns, and their lower branches remain on the trunk all the way to the ground, drooping and turning up at the ends. On favorable locations, height growth may be as much as 18 inches in one season. The wide variety of sites and soils on which it will grow, the tree's fast growth and its symmetrical form make white spruce one of the most favored conifers for landscape planting. Nearly a dozen nursery varieties of this species are available. White spruce is also planted in many localities for Christmas tree production.

The bark of white spruce is orange-brown on the young twigs, becoming brown on the branches and finally ash-gray on the old trunk, where it is broken into small, thin, scaly plates. The inner bark is flesh-colored or pinkish, whereas that of the black spruce is olive-green. Due to the pitchy nature of the bark and foliage, white spruce is easily damaged by light fires.

Crushed white spruce needles have an unpleasant odor that accounts for the names "cat spruce" and "skunk spruce" sometimes heard. Four-angled in cross section, $\frac{1}{3}$- to $\frac{2}{3}$-inch long, sharp-pointed and stiff, the needles frequently appear to be massed on the upper side of the twig because of their curvature, though actually they grow from all sides of the twig. They

persist for seven to 10 years, leaving raised, rough bases on the twigs when they fall. Color of the needles varies from dark green to bluish green, according to the amount of bloom or whitish cast, which differs somewhat from one tree to the next. The buds are broadly rounded and blunt, $\frac{1}{8}$- to $\frac{1}{4}$-inch long, and light brown in color.

Flowers appear in May and early June. Pale red staminate flowers form in long-stalked clusters near the ends of the twigs and the red-scaled ovulate flowers form in oblong clusters near the top of the tree. The cones are mature by the end of the summer and fall off shortly after the seeds are discharged in autumn. Clay-brown in color and one to two or more inches long, the oblong, pendent cones are composed of eight to 12 spirally arranged rows of flexible, lustrous scales which are rounded and smooth on the margins. The light brown seeds are about $\frac{1}{8}$-inch long with wings about $\frac{1}{4}$- to $\frac{3}{8}$-inch long. One pound of cleaned seed will contain as many as 230,000 seeds.

As with black spruce and balsam, the greatest enemy of white spruce, other than fire, is the spruce budworm. While pure spruce stands are normally not attacked, spruce may be seriously damaged where it occurs with old balsam which is actually the preferred host. The spruce bark beetles and carpenter ants frequently attack scarred or weakened trees. Cut logs left in exposed, sunny places are readily attacked by wood sawyer beetles whose larvae tunnel into the wood, frequently rendering it useless for commercial purposes. Certain wood rots and rusts are common in both black and white spruce, but seldom cause widespread damage.

Areas in Michigan in which white spruce predominates are so few and small that this acreage generally is lumped with that of other species in classifications of forest areas. Nearly all of the commercial volume of white spruce is located in the Upper Peninsula.

The wood of white spruce is pale yellow in color, straight-grained, soft, weak, and weighs only 28 pounds per cubic foot when dry. It warps very little. Besides its principal use for pulpwood, it is used also in general construction work and for interior finish, boats and canoes, oars and paddles, sounding boards for musical instruments, and woodenware.

Identifying characteristics: Needles $\frac{1}{4}$- to $\frac{3}{4}$-inch long, four-angled, unpleasantly odorous; cones oblong, one to two inches long, scales lustrous, margins smooth; bark scaly, inner bark pinkish.

BLACK SPRUCE

Picea mariana (Mill.) B. S. P.

BLACK SPRUCE IS TYPICAL OF OUR COLD northern swamps, often enduring situations where other trees will not grow. It was at one time an important source of pulpwood for paper manufacture, and should be familiar to everyone in Michigan for it is the most common of our native Christmas trees.

One of the seven species of spruce native to North America, it is one of two found in Michigan, the other being white spruce, with which it is frequently associated in its northern range.

Black spruce seldom occurs in the south part of the Lower Peninsula. In the north part of the Lower Peninsula and in the Upper Peninsula it occurs mainly in poorly drained, low, wet pockets and in sphagnum swamps. It may be associated with white spruce, balsam, tamarack, cedar and swamp hardwoods; or it may grow in pure, dense stands. In the extreme north it may be found on comparatively dry soils coming in under aspen or even jack pine. Areas of virgin black spruce still exist in the Upper Peninsula.

Best growth is attained on well-drained, bottom land soils. On poorly drained acid bogs growth is exceedingly slow, trees occasionally attaining a diameter of only three or four inches in 100 years. Like other spruces, this species is very tolerant of shade, and after enduring long periods of suppression, will grow well when released.

Normally only a small- to medium-sized tree 40 to 50 feet tall and six to 12 inches in diameter at maturity, black spruce under favorable conditions has been known to reach 100 feet in height and three feet in diameter. Ages of 200 years are not uncommon. Its slender, tapering trunk is supported by a shallow root system easily damaged by fire, and in swamps and bogs it is easily uprooted by strong winds. The crowns of young trees are spire-shaped, though not so symmetrical nor sharp-pointed as the balsam. Old forest-grown trees have narrow, open crowns, while open-grown trees have spreading, solid crowns. Branches are short, the younger ones ascending slightly, the older drooping and turning up at the ends. The lower branches persist for m a n y y e a r s after dying, making the tree unattractive for ornamental use.

Bark on young twigs is at first green, then reddish, covered with fine, rust-colored hairs. On the old branches and trunk it is gray-brown to reddish brown, scaly and resinous. The olive-green color of the inner bark serves to distinguish this tree quickly from white spruce, which has pinkish inner bark.

Needles of black spruce are ¼- to ¾-inch long, four-sided in cross section, dark green to bluish green, blunt-pointed and stiff.

Growing from all sides of the twig, they remain on the branches for seven or eight years leaving raised, woody bases on the twigs when they fall. When crushed they produce a pleasing pitchy odor. The buds are ovoid, pointed, about ⅛-inch long, light reddish brown in color, and finely woolly.

Flowers appear in May and early June, the staminate round with dark red anthers, the ovulate oblong with rounded purple scales. Cones form in the late summer or fall of the first year, but may remain on the branches only partly opened for several years. One-half to 1-inch long, they are oval and pointed when closed but nearly round when open, and narrowed at the base into a short, incurved stock. The rigid scales are gray-brown, rounded and ragged on the margin. Seeds are dark brown, about ⅛-inch long with wings that measure ¼- to ⅜-inch. About 500,000 cleaned seeds weigh one pound. Seed dispersal takes place throughout the entire year.

Spruce budworm outbreaks are important in black spruce stands where old-growth balsam is present for the infestation first builds up on the preferred balsam. While attacks of this insect frequently are not fatal to the spruce, they are often followed by infestations of the spruce bark beetle which complete the destruction of weakened and dying trees. Dwarf mistletoe, a parasitic plant which causes the growth deformity known as "witches-broom," results in eventual mortality and is considered a threat to black spruce stands.

Commercially, black and white spruce are not separated. Both yield pulp of high quality and are equally desirable for most purposes. Nearly 90 percent of the commercial stands of black spruce is in the Upper Peninsula.

The wood of black spruce is soft, pale yellow in color, with thin white sapwood. It is light in weight, averaging only 28 pounds per cubic foot when dry. Because of its generally small size, compared with white spruce, little or no black spruce is sawed into lumber, the bulk of it going into pulp for the manufacture of high-grade papers. Other uses include mine timbers, piano sounding boards and woodenware. Large numbers of small black spruce trees are cut for Christmas trees. Amber pitch which collects in hard masses on wounds in the bark is sold commercially as spruce gum.

Identifying characteristics: Needles ¼- to ¾-inch long, four-angled; cones rounded when open, ½- to 1-inch long, scale margins ragged; bark scaly, inner bark olive-green; commonly found in swamps and bogs in northern Michigan.

13

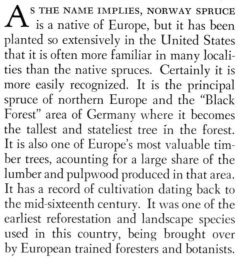

NORWAY SPRUCE

Picea abies (L.) Karst.

As the name implies, Norway spruce is a native of Europe, but it has been planted so extensively in the United States that it is often more familiar in many localities than the native spruces. Certainly it is more easily recognized. It is the principal spruce of northern Europe and the "Black Forest" area of Germany where it becomes the tallest and stateliest tree in the forest. It is also one of Europe's most valuable timber trees, acounting for a large share of the lumber and pulpwood produced in that area. It has a record of cultivation dating back to the mid-sixteenth century. It was one of the earliest reforestation and landscape species used in this country, being brought over by European trained foresters and botanists.

Norway spruce has been planted throughout Michigan and is a favorite tree for parks, estates, farm yards, cemeteries, windbreaks, shelterbelts, and hedges. It has been planted in the past for reforestation, but has been replaced by native species for this purpose. It is finding increasing favor, however, as a plantation grown Christmas tree, and many thousands are marketed annually. Easy to transplant, it makes its best growth on rich, moist soils, but does well on a variety of sites. It grows more rapidly than our native spruces, but is not as hardy, occasionally suffering from late frosts and drought. Ordinarily in this locality it grows to 60 or 70 (occasionally 100) feet in height and one to two feet in diameter; while in its native regions it may reach 150 feet in height and five feet in diameter. Such sizes made it very valuable at one time as masts for the great ocean sailing ships.

Young Norway spruce trees have a pleasing conical or spire-like form, with drooping or upsweeping branches and characteristic pendulous branchlets which distinguish it at a glance from other spruces. As the trees mature the crowns and foliage thin out giving a ragged, unkempt look.

The bark on the young twigs is orange and smooth at first, turning reddish brown and roughened on the small branches. On young trunks it is light-brown with thin, papery scales, and on old trunks gray-brown with thick scales. The bark exudes a pitch known as "Burgundy pitch" in Europe where it is used in varnishes and medicines.

Norway spruce needles are dark green and lustrous, and have a fragrant, pitchy odor when crushed. They are ½ to ¾ inch long, stiff, curved, and sharp pointed, square or slightly flattened in cross-section. Arranged spirally on the twigs, they remain for five to seven years leaving short peg-like bases when they fall.

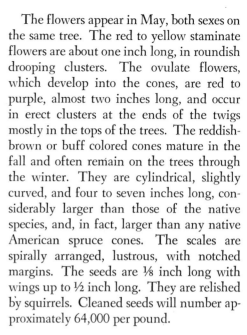

The flowers appear in May, both sexes on the same tree. The red to yellow staminate flowers are about one inch long, in roundish drooping clusters. The ovulate flowers, which develop into the cones, are red to purple, almost two inches long, and occur in erect clusters at the ends of the twigs mostly in the tops of the trees. The reddish-brown or buff colored cones mature in the fall and often remain on the trees through the winter. They are cylindrical, slightly curved, and four to seven inches long, considerably larger than those of the native species, and, in fact, larger than any native American spruce cones. The scales are spirally arranged, lustrous, with notched margins. The seeds are ⅛ inch long with wings up to ½ inch long. They are relished by squirrels. Cleaned seeds will number approximately 64,000 per pound.

The same insects and diseases which attack native spruces may also work on Norway spruce, although attacks by certain pests typical of forest conditions are not as common. One of the insects which causes most concern on ornamental trees and in Christmas tree plantations is the eastern spruce gall aphid which produces a small pineapple shaped growth at the base of the new shoots, often killing them. Heavy or repeated infestations may seriously weaken or deform the trees. The larvae of the white pine weevil cause damage in young trees by mining in the terminal twigs, killing them and often resulting in a poorly formed tree. Other pests include spruce needle miners, sawflies and red spiders. A canker disease may cause the death of large branches.

The wood of Norway spruce is white or buff colored, strong, tough and straight grained. It is soft, easily worked, and very light, weighing only 25 pounds per cubic foot when dry. Its long fibers and lack of resin make it ideal for paper pulp which is its principal use in Europe. Spruce pulp is one of Scandinavia's major exports, with considerable quantities reaching paper mills in eastern United States. Other uses include wood carvings and clocks, musical instruments, toys, and lumber for boxes, crates and construction work.

Identifying characteristics: Needles ½ to ¾ inch long, four angled, slightly flattened; cones cylindrical, 4 to 7 inches long, scale margins notched; branches up-sweeping, twigs pendulous; bark gray-brown, scaly.

HEMLOCK

Tsuga canadensis (L.) Carr.

SINCE THE TURN OF THE CENTURY hemlock has maintained a significant place in the forests of northern Michigan, although it is dwindling in both importance and abundance. Generally ignored during the pine cutting era, or cut only for its bark and left in the woods to rot, it gradually assumed prominence as other species became scarce. Though heavily cut, it still accounts for 50 percent of the total softwood lumber production, and 5 percent of the total lumber production of all species in the state. In addition it furnishes pulpwood used in Michigan's pulp and paper manufacture and its bark is still the main source of natural tannin for the leather industry. Michigan is the leading producer of eastern hemlock lumber.

One of the four species of hemlock found in the United States, and the only one native to Michigan, the eastern hemlock occurs only occasionally in the south half of the Lower Peninsula, increasing in abundance northward, becoming more plentiful in the extreme northern and northwestern counties of the Lower Peninsula and the east half of the Upper Peninsula, reaching its greatest abundance in the vast hardwood forest areas of the west end of the Upper Peninsula.

Hemlock seldom forms pure stands, but usually occurs in mixture with such other species as white pine, maple, beech, yellow birch, balsam, basswood and elm, forming one of the principal trees of the so-called "hardwood-hemlock" association. One of the most shade-resistant coniferous species, it is able to withstand the dense shade of hardwood forests under which it may grow slowly for 100 years or more before piercing the overtopping canopy. Found on a variety of sites, it makes its best growth on cool moist soils typical of the hardwood forest. Hemlocks well over 100 feet in height and four or more feet in diameter are occasionally found, although heights for mature trees run usually 60 to 80 feet with diameters of two to three feet. Trees of this species over 600 years old have been found, but maturity is usually reached in 150 to 200 years.

The ragged crown of large hemlocks is supported by a shallow spreading root system and a massive trunk which holds its taper well for nearly two-thirds of its height, losing it rapidly above this point. The spreading branches are tipped with gracefully drooping, flexible shoots which tend to curve away from the direction of the prevailng winds. Dead branches often persist for many years, the slow growth of the wood around them forming exceedingly hard, flint-like knots. Small open-grown trees are graceful in outline with dense pyramidal crowns, making them very desirable for ornamental plantings.

On young hemlocks the bark is smooth to flaky and light purplish brown in color. On mature trees it is rough, deeply grooved, two to three inches thick, dark cinnamon-brown in color. The needles are 1/3- to 2/3-inch long, flat, rounded or slightly notched at the end, remaining on the branches for two or three years. Dark yellow-green and shiny on the upper surface, they are light green, marked with two parallel whitish lines beneath. Like balsam needles, they tend to lie in a flat spray although actually arranged spirally along the twigs.

Flowers occur in May, the small yellow staminate ones in the axils of the previous season's leaves; and the erect greenish ovulate ones at the ends of the twigs. The cones, maturing in September and October, are purplish brown, oval, pointed, about ¾-inch long, and hang loosely on the twigs. The two small winged seeds, borne at the base of each scale, are scattered during the winter, providing food for birds. Each seed is about 1/16-inch long, nearly 200,000 being required to make a pound. While an abundance of seed is produced every two or three years, the species does not reproduce well since the young seedlings are very delicate.

Wind, lightning and fire cause most of the losses in eastern hemlock timber, although an insect known as the hemlock looper is capable of doing considerable damage in Michigan. Large hemlocks are susceptible to "ring-shake"—a longitudinal splitting along an annual growth ring which results in low-grade lumber. Because of its shallow root system this species is easily damaged or killed by light surface fires which burn leaves and humus.

Although cheaper and inferior to pine for ordinary building purposes, hemlock lumber increases in demand as prices of other species go up. The light reddish-brown wood is soft, brittle, splintery, and not durable when exposed to the weather. A cubic foot of seasoned hemlock weighs 28 pounds. Its principal uses in Michigan are for lumber, boxes and crates, ties, mine timbers, lath, and pulp. Paper made from hemlock pulp is used largely for newsprint and wrapping papers.

Identifying characteristics: Needles 1/3- to 2/3-inch long, two parallel whitish lines beneath; twigs soft, flexible; cones ¾-inch long, pendant; bark cinnamon-brown, rough, deeply fissured on large trees; trunk tapering rapidly in the crown.

15

BALSAM FIR

Abies balsamea (L.) Mill.

TYPICALLY A COLD CLIMATE TREE, BALsam fir is found abundantly in northern Michigan, particularly in the Upper Peninsula, and only occasionally in the extreme southern part of the state, inhabiting swamps and adjacent flats and moist slopes. Of the 10 species of fir native to the United States, only two are found east of the Rocky Mountains—our common balsam, and a similar but relatively unimportant species found high in the southern Appalachian mountains.

Requiring abundant moisture for best development, balsam fir attains its largest size around swamp borders on rather poorly drained ground, where it is usually associated with black or white spruce, aspen, and white birch, or occasionally forms small pure patches. It may occur nearly pure in swamps, or mixed with cedar, spruce and tamarack. Occasionally it appears with upland hardwoods, or on drier, sandy soils with the pines, if there is ample shade.

Balsam is ordinarily a small to medium-sized tree of 40 to 60 feet at maturity, with diameters ranging from 12 to occasionally 18 inches. It is comparatively short-lived, trees over 90 years old being rarely found. The crown of balsam is sharp pointed, slender and symmetrical, large trees having a spire-like appearance, widest at the base, tapering gradually upward. The slender trunk is supported by a shallow, spreading root system. Branching occurs in whorls of four to six about the main stem, with dead branches around the base of the tree persisting for many years.

Characteristically dotted with balsam pitch blisters, the bark on young trees is thin, rather smooth, dull gray-green, later becoming ash-gray with scattered light patches. On old trees the bark becomes grayish brown and roughened by fine irregular scales.

Balsam needles, arranged spirally on the twigs although often appearing to be in two rows, vary in size and shape on different parts of the tree. Those on the lower sterile side branches are the longest, being 1- to 1½-inches long. Soft, flattened, blunt or often notched at the ends, they tend to lie in a horizontal plane. On the upper, cone-producing branches they are ½- to 1-inch long, rather sharp pointed, thick and firm, tending to curve upward over the twig. Dark green and lustrous on the upper surface, the needles are pale green, marked with two parallel whitish lines or grooves on the under surface. They are a favorite food of moose and are eaten to some extent by deer. A refreshing pitchy odor is produced when the needles are crushed. They remain on the twigs for many years, leaving a small flat scar when they fall.

Cones occur annually in the topmost branches of the tree, in large trees forming dense purple clusters visible from quite a distance. Two to four inches long, the oval cones sit upright on the branches, disintegrating rapidly after becoming ripe in September and October, when the thin, flexible cone scales fall away leaving the central woody spike still standing on the stem. The seeds are about ¼-inch long with broad, purplish-brown wings. It requires approximately 50,000 cleaned seeds to make a pound. Abundant seed is produced every two to three years, but relatively few of the seeds germinate even when planted in a nursery. Despite this fact, balsam reproduction is usually very plentiful near seed trees in swamps and moist shaded woods.

The most serious enemy of balsam fir, other than fire, is the spruce budworm. In stands in which balsam and spruce are the predominating species, this insect often becomes epidemic, killing these trees over large areas. From 1910 to 1925 the budworm destroyed millions of cords of balsam in the Northeast and Lake States where this species had become abundant following the removal of pine. Weakened and dying trees, as well as cut logs which are left in the woods, are readily attacked by wood boring insects, particularly the balsam fir sawyer which leaves deposits of sawdust-like chaff around bases of trees or logs. Live trees are frequently attacked and killed by the mottled bark disease which causes a red rot in the heart-wood, and commercial losses from butt rot are large. Balsam is very susceptible to drought injury and to changes in soil water levels.

Balsam is a favorite Christmas tree, and one which holds its needles remarkably well. Thousands of small balsams are cut annually as part of Michigan's large Christmas tree industry.

The wood of balsam fir is light, pale brown, frequently streaked with yellow, weak, soft, coarse grained and quickly perishable. A cubic foot of dry balsam wood weighs 25 pounds. Its principal uses in Michigan are lumber, box and crate stock, pulpwood and cabin logs. Oil of fir, or "Canada balsam," a clear liquid resin which is distilled from both the bark and needles, is used in pharmaceutical compounds and in mounting lenses and covers on microscope slides.

Identifying characteristics: Needles aromatic, more or less flattened, ½- to 1¼-inches long, two whitish parallel lines on underside; bark ash-gray, smooth, containing pitch blisters; tip of tree spire-like.

WHITE CEDAR or ARBORVITAE   *Thuja occidentalis* L.

ONE OF THE TWO SPECIES OF THE GENUS *Thuja* native to North America, white cedar, or arborvitae as it is commonly called, is found abundantly in the swamps of northeastern United States. The other species occurs in the Pacific Northwest. In Michigan white cedar grows throughout the Upper Peninsula and in the Lower Peninsula seldom farther south than Montcalm and Lapeer counties. In addition to the great commercial value of its wide variety of wood uses, it is the most important winter food of Michigan's large deer herd, and its dense stands are used extensively as winter deer yards. So important is this food that winter starvation is common in those areas where it has been browsed out. Native white cedar, as well as the many exotic and horticultural varieties, is widely planted for hedges, windrows, and landscape purposes. The name "arborvitae," meaning "tree of life," may have been given to this species by the early French voyageurs who learned from the Indians its value in treating scurvy, a common affliction of sailors and explorers lacking vitamin C in their diets.

Preferring cold, wet sites with slow drainage, but not stagnant water, white cedar frequently forms almost impenetrable pure stands in swamps and on low stream borders; or it occurs in mixture with black spruce, balsam and tamarack, and with swamp-hardwood species such as black ash, white birch, red maple and balm-of-Gilead. Occasionally it is found with white pine, hemlock and yellow birch on heavy, moist soils. Pure, even-aged stands, reproducing heavily following cutting, frequently remain for many years in a stagnated condition, and require as much as 100 years to grow an inch in diameter. Growth is slow even under good conditions, 10 to 20 years being required to grow an inch in diameter. Fires may completely change the composition of cedar swamps, allowing willow and tag alder to come in, often to the exclusion of the cedar.

Ordinarily a tree of only 40 or 50 feet in height with a diameter of 2- to 2½-feet at maturity, white cedar occasionally reaches a height of 70 feet or more and a diameter of four feet. Frequently twisted, leaning, or even lying flat on the ground at the base, the tapering trunk supports a rather dense pyramidal crown of short, stiff, more or less horizontal branches. The root system is shallow and spreading, roots occurring often above the ground surface for a short distance from the tree. The thin bark is light yellow-brown on the twigs, becoming reddish on the small branches, and finally light grayish brown on the trunk, where it is divided into shallowly grooved, narrow, horizontal, fibrous strips which tend to spiral around the trunk.

The minute, appressed, scale-like leaves occur in ranks of four, the top and bottom leaves flat, and the two side leaves folded. The leaf groups overlap one another tightly, appearing collectively as a flat fan-like spray. Dark green and lustrous on the upper surface, the leaf shoots are lighter green and dull beneath, and are pleasingly aromatic when crushed. They are persistent for one or two years only.

The flowers occur in April and May, the ovulate in conspicuous purple clusters, the staminate yellow and inconspicuous. Cones appear in early autumn and persist throughout the winter. They are short-stalked, erect, about ½-inch long, light brown and oval shaped, composed of four to six pairs of papery scales. The winged seeds are about ⅛-inch long, numbering 250,000 to 300,000 per pound.

Butt rot causes a considerable loss in merchantable cedar and is perhaps its most serious disease. Among the insects attacking the foliage two are rather common in Michigan, although neither has been sufficiently abundant to cause serious damage. These are the arborvitae leaf-miner which feeds in and kills terminal shoots, but seldom seriously damages the tree; and the bag worm which defoliates and occasionally kills trees. Perhaps the most serious pest is the carpenter ant which attacks the wood. Entering through a wound or rotting place near the base of the tree, colonies of these ants completely riddle the heartwood in the butt, rendering it useless.

The fragrant wood of white cedar is soft, straight-grained and brittle, and can be split into thin, straight pieces. It is light in weight, a cubic foot of seasoned wood weighing only 22 pounds. The sapwood is white, the heartwood light yellow-brown. Its durability in contact with moisture gives it its wide variety of uses, principal of which in Michigan are fence posts, vineyard posts, guard rails, telephone poles, ties, shingles, cabin logs, mine timbers, rustic furniture and lumber. Fence posts alone account for 60 percent of the annual harvest. Mine timbers account for nearly 20 percent. Cedar lumber is produced in small quantities and is used principally for interior paneling.

Identifying characteristics: Leaves minute, scale-like, aromatic, in fan-like sprays; cones ½-inch long, erect; bark grayish brown, thin and fibrous; common in northern swamps.

17

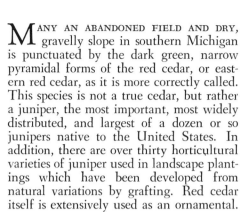

RED CEDAR

Juniperus virginiana L.

MANY AN ABANDONED FIELD AND DRY, gravelly slope in southern Michigan is punctuated by the dark green, narrow pyramidal forms of the red cedar, or eastern red cedar, as it is more correctly called. This species is not a true cedar, but rather a juniper, the most important, most widely distributed, and largest of a dozen or so junipers native to the United States. In addition, there are over thirty horticultural varieties of juniper used in landscape plantings which have been developed from natural variations by grafting. Red cedar itself is extensively used as an ornamental.

Red cedar wood should be familiar to everyone, for it is the wood most commonly used in cedar chests and cedar closets. Its former use for pencils has given this tree the name "pencil" cedar in many localities. The demand for this purpose dates back to colonial days and became so great that the available supply of good timber has almost disappeared. Most of the present commercial production comes from Tennessee, Kentucky, Virginia and the Carolinas.

In Michigan red cedar is confined almost entirely to the southern half of the Lower Peninsula where it is most often seen in dry abandoned fields and pastures, along fence rows, and on open hillsides. Gravelly moraines and soils of limestone origin seem to be favored. Although very drought resistant and usually associated with areas of low moisture and fertility, it is also found on lake and stream borders, and makes its best development on rich bottom land soils.

In some parts of its range, red cedar has been known to attain a height of 100 feet and a diameter of four feet. In Michigan, however, it seldom grows larger than 40 or 50 feet tall and 12 to 18 inches in diameter. When growing in the open it is usually a small straight tree with ascending branches which start nearly at the ground. Dense pyramidal, oval or columnar forms are typical of young trees, and the crowns become more open and irregular with age. It is extremely slow growing and lives to be 200 to 300 years old.

The bark on the twigs is greenish to reddish brown and smooth. On the larger branches and trunk it is a light reddish brown, thin and fibrous, separating in vertical shreds and turning gray with age. The smooth, reddish inner bark is often exposed, and this tree was called "baton rouge" or "red stick" by early French settlers who found it growing in Louisiana and named a city, now the state capital, after it.

One of the unusual characteristics of red cedar is the two forms of leaves it possesses. One form is ¼- to ½-inch long, sharp pointed and awl-shaped. This form occurs on the seedlings and vigorous young shoots. The other kind, only 1/16 of an inch across, are ridged scales occurring in overlapping, opposite pairs on the old growth.

The leaves remain on the trees for five or six years and are dark green at first, gradually turning to brown. The winter buds are very small and inconspicuous.

The minute flowers appear in May, the two sexes usually on different trees. The staminate are small cones composed of four to six thin scales; the ovulate are in rounded clusters and composed of three pairs of fleshy, blue scales.

The fruit matures in the autumn of the first or second year. While technically a cone, it is actually a dark blue, fleshy, pea-sized berry containing one or two (rarely three or four) small brown seeds which number 18,000 to 30,000 to a pound. The berries have a powdery coating which makes them appear whitish. They are persistent on the tree the year around and are known to be eaten by over fifty different kinds of birds, which is the principal means by which the seeds are scattered. The alcohol used in making gin is distilled over this and other species of juniper berries to give it its distinctive flavor.

The principal enemy of the red cedar is fire. Its thin shreddy bark makes it an easy prey for even light grass fires. The junipers are affected by the cedar-apple rust which causes great damage in certain localities to commercial apple crops. The rust spends part of its life cycle on the juniper, which is often damaged or killed, and the other part on apples or closely related species like hawthorn. Rust spores may spread from the juniper to apple orchards a mile or two away.

Red cedar wood is soft, brittle, moderately strong, with a fine, even grain. It is extremely durable in contact with the soil. When freshly cut it is pinkish to deep red or purple in color, gradually turning to dull light brown upon exposure. It can be easily worked and takes a high polish. A cubic foot of seasoned wood weighs 33 pounds. Its odor is distinctive and is one of the surest means of identification.

In addition to pencils and cedar chests, red cedar is used in cigar boxes, canoes, woodenware, caskets, veneers, interior finish, and scientific instruments. Small trees are frequently cut for fence posts and it is a common Christmas tree in the South. Cedar oil which is distilled from wood chips and also from leaves and twigs is used to flavor medicines, perfumes and soaps. The wood oil has a high index of refraction and is used in the preparation of permanent microscope mounts.

Identifying characteristics: Leaves minute, on young shoots awl-shaped, on old growth overlapping, scale-like; bark thin, shreddy, inner bark reddish; fruit a pea-sized blue berry with whitish bloom; young trees pyramidal; southern Michigan, on dry sites.

BLACK WILLOW

Salix nigra Marsh.

THE IDENTIFICATION OF THE VARIOUS willows is a real task even for the specialist. Botanists recognize more than 170 tree and shrub species, with enough natural and cultivated varieties and hybrids to bring the total to nearly 300.

Willows are found over most of the cooler parts of the northern hemisphere, with dwarfed forms extending into the Arctic regions as far as plant life exists. Most of the species are shrubby in habit, only 25 of the 65 North American kinds attaining tree size. About 30 species of willow trees and shrubs occur in Michigan, some of them of foreign origin but more or less naturalized. Among them is the familiar and graceful "weeping willow," an exotic from Asia, with long, pendent branches and light green foliage. Another well known species is that delightful herald of spring, the "pussy willow." The most common native tree of this species in Michigan and throughout North America is the black willow, a description of which will serve to represent the group.

As timber producers the willows are relatively unimportant. However, their value in landscaping, as windbreaks and in soil and bank erosion control gives them a definite place among our more useful plants. Their importance as game food cannot be overlooked for the winter buds are commonly eaten by partridge and sharp-tailed grouse as well as by other birds, while the young bark and shoots are fed on by rabbits and deer.

Black willow occurs throughout the state usually along water courses and lakes, or in other places where abundant moisture is available for its shallow root system. It is a rapid growing and short-lived tree, maturing in 50 to 70 years but often living considerably longer. Full grown trees may be only 40 to 50 feet in height and 20 inches in diameter with single stems, or they may attain much greater proportions with trunks up to four feet in diameter, often dividing near the base into large diverging branches, forming a broad, irregular, round-topped crown. Not competitive by nature, black willow usually occurs in the open as a solitary tree or in pure clusters or groves.

The slender young branches are very flexible but are brittle at the base, often breaking off in ice or wind storms. Many willows along rivers have developed from small broken branches which were carried downstream and became imbedded in the bank, sprouting and growing into large trees. The prolific sprouting ability of willows makes propagation by branch cuttings the easiest means of reproduction. Shelter belt and erosion control plantings are established by this means.

The bark on young black willow twigs is reddish to orange or greenish brown in color, smooth and shiny. On the older branches it becomes light brown, finally turning dark brown to black on the main branches

and trunk. Old trunks have long, connected, irregular ridges which are often scaly or stringy. The fissures between the ridges are deep and angular. A bitter concoction made from the bark was at one time used for the treatment of fevers.

The narrow, finely-toothed leaves are alternate, three to six inches long, ½- to 1-inch wide, with a shiny green upper surface and a dull, grayish green underside. They are lance-shaped, tapering to a sharp tip, and more or less rounded at the base. The leaf stem is short; and where it joins the twig is found a pair of small leaf-like appendages or bracts. The winter buds are reddish brown, ⅛- to $\frac{1}{16}$-inch long and sharp pointed, hugging the stem tightly. Each bud is covered by a single bud scale.

The willows are among the first trees to flower in the spring, the minute blossoms appearing before the leaves, with the staminate and pistillate catkins on separate trees. The mature seeds, contained in slender cone-shaped capsules along the female catkins, are minute and cottony, and are widely scattered by the wind. Because of the abundance of these fluffy seeds the female tree is less desirable for lawn purposes.

Willow is subject to numerous insects and diseases which attack all parts of the tree, usually with only minor effects. Among these are: "tar spot," a fungus which causes raised black spots on the leaves; several leaf rusts and gall-making insects; the poplar borer; and fungi which cause decay in the branches and trunk.

Black willow furnishes most of the small quantity of willow lumber which reaches commercial channels, the principal producing area being in the lower Mississippi Valley. The character of the wood and the crooked nature of the logs make it undesirable for most uses. While the wood is soft, it is tough, flexible, and fairly strong. It is light in weight, a cubic foot of dry wood weighing only 26 pounds. Its color is light reddish brown, often streaked. Willow is not durable in contact with the soil.

Very little willow lumber is produced in Michigan. Here as elsewhere the lumber is used mostly in boxes and crates. It has important uses in other forms, however. Its flexibility and resistance to splitting combined with its light weight make it ideal for artificial limbs for which it is the preferred wood. It is also the best wood for polo balls. In certain areas it is an important pulpwood species. The shoots of various species of willow are used the world over for making baskets and wicker furniture.

Identifying characteristics: Leaves alternate, lance-shaped, three to six inches long, ½- to 1-inch wide, margins toothed; leaf-like bracts at base of leaf stem; buds with single scale; twigs slender, flexible, smooth with reddish to orange or greenish-brown bark; old trunks brown to black with long connected ridges and deep fissures.

QUAKING ASPEN

Populus tremuloides Michx.

ONE OF MICHIGAN'S MOST IMPORTANT trees from the standpoint of forestry and game is the quaking aspen, known also as trembling aspen, smalltooth aspen, or "popple." While typically associated with northern Michigan, this species occurs throughout the state, and, in fact, bears the distinction of having the most extensive range of any tree in North America being found throughout northeastern United States, nearly all of Canada, west to Alaska, and south through western United States to northern Mexico. It also grows on a greater variety of sites than any other tree, occuring on dry stands with jack pine as well as in wet tamarack swamps.

As a "pioneer" species or reclaimer of cut-over and burned-over land, quaking aspen together with its common associate, the largetooth aspen, make up the principal forest cover on nearly five million acres of Michigan's 19 million acres of forest land. The quaking aspen provides shade and improves the soil for maple, pine, balsam and other tolerant species which gradually come into such stands. Popple thickets provide excellent game cover, and new popple sprouts, as well as twigs in tree tops cut in logging operations, are important winter deer food. Aspen buds are a favorite winter food of ruffed grouse.

Quaking aspen is generally found in even-aged stands, either pure or in mixture with other species. Under forest conditions it produces a straight slender trunk normally 50 to 60 feet high and eight to 12 inches in diameter at maturity, with a small, rounded crown of slender, brittle branches. Trees measuring 18 inches in diameter and 70 to 80 feet high are not uncommon in certain parts of the Upper Peninsula. Like the other poplars, it is intolerant of shade and easily crowded out by shade-producing trees. Generally short-lived, decay may be common in stands only 40 years old on poor sites, through 50 to 60 years is its normal life span.

The bark on the twigs is reddish brown and shiny, becoming whitish to yellow-green and more or less roughened by horizontal, black, warty lines on the larger branches and trunk. The base of the trunk on old trees becomes fissured and nearly black. Despite its bitter taste, the bark is one of the principal foods of the beaver.

The slightest breeze will set the small, rounded or nearly heart-shaped leaves of the quaking aspen in motion, producing a rustling sound. Arranged alternately on the twigs, the finely-toothed leaves are 1½- to 2½-inches across, dark green above, paler beneath. The petioles or leaf stems are flattened with the widest part next to the leaf. The flowers appear before the leaves in the spring in hanging catkins with the pollen-bearing and seed-producing flowers on separate trees. The fruit, maturing in May and June, is a small capsule containing minute, brown, hairy seeds easily scattered by the wind. Large areas may be seeded by this species where mineral soil is exposed. Reproduction also occurs from root sprouting stimulated by fires or cutting of parent trees.

The terminal winter buds are about ½-inch long, sharp pointed, with a varnished appearance. The lateral buds are curved in toward the stem.

The forest tent caterpillar is the most destructive insect that attacks the aspen, and heavy infestations of this pest occur periodically causing widespread defoliation. Tree trunks may be nearly covered with these worms. While the trees usually produce a second set of leaves the same year, repeated defoliations will weaken and occasionally kill them. Weakened trees are easy prey for other insects and diseases. Wood borers sometimes riddle the wood, making it weak and worthless. *Hypoxylon* canker is an important disease affecting the stems of all age classes, young stands sometimes losing a quarter of the trees. Wood decay caused by the bracket fungus, *Fomes igniarius,* accounts for a major loss in wood volume.

Commercially, largetooth and quaking aspen are grouped together and make up approximately 15 percent of the total cubic foot volume of timber in the state. Approximately 50 percent of this volume lies in the north half of the Lower Peninsula, five percent in the south half and the balance in the Upper Peninsula. Unlike most other species in Michigan, the annual growth of aspen exceeds the annual drain; thus the supply is steadily increasing. The rapid growth and the large potential supply coupled with their wildlife value have brought the aspens into prominence.

Nearly identical, the woods of quaking aspen and largetooth aspen are uniform in texture, nearly white to light brown in color, soft and weak, weighing 26 pounds per cubic foot when air-dry. Green aspen lumber has a characteristic disagreeable odor which disappears when it is seasoned. The principal uses are pulp for book and magazine papers, hardboard, lumber, pallets, crating, matches, excelsior, food containers, furniture core stock, interior trim, toys, and unpainted furniture.

Identifying characteristics: Leaves alternate, nearly round with a small tip, fine toothed; leaf stem flattened; winter buds ½-inch long, shiny, sharp pointed, lateral buds incurred; bark whitish to yellow-green, smoooth on young trees with warty horizontal lines, on old trees blackened and furrowed near base.

LARGETOOTH ASPEN

Populus grandidentata Michx.

L ARGETOOTH ASPEN IS ONE OF FOUR common species of poplar native to Michigan. It is more often called just "aspen" or "popple" along with its close relative and companion, the smalltooth or quaking aspen. The importance of these two species in reclaiming cut-over and burned-over land in northern Michigan has been great. Large areas in the Lake States and other regions would be treeless but for these "weed species," so-called because of their prolific nature, rapid growth and relatively short life. More desirable species such as white pine, spruce and balsam frequently come in under the protective cover of the aspens.

The occurrence of largetooth aspen in Michigan is principally in the north half of the Lower Peninsula but it is also found in the Upper Peninsula where it reaches very large size. It grows best on rich, moist, sandy soils but is more common on cut-over and burned-over sandy hills of low fertility where it may be found in association with quaking aspen, red maple, red and white oaks, white birch, and red, white and jack pines. Pure stands are common over extensive areas where it seeded following fires. Preferring the open, it will not thrive in shade or under intense competition.

Normally a small tree of 12 to 15 inches in diameter and 40 to 50 feet high, largetooth aspen occasionally attains two feet in diameter and 70 feet in height. Deterioration in the trunk begins at a fairly early age, varying with the growing conditions, 50 to 60 years being its average life span.

Under crowded forest conditions, this species has a slender trunk and a small, oval or rounded, rather open crown with slender brittle branches. The bark is olive or light brownish green in color, smooth on young stems, becoming marked on older trunks with characteristic wedge-shaped branch scars in the upper part, and is furrowed and gray near the ground. The terminal winter buds are about ¼-inch long, conical in shape, pointed and covered with a dusty coating. The lateral buds point out from the twigs at an acute angle.

The leaves of largetooth aspen are densely woolly and dusty-white when first appearing in the spring, later becoming dark yellow-green and smooth. They are three to five inches long, about two-thirds as wide, slightly pointed and broadly rounded at the base. The margins are broken with coarse, rounded teeth, frequently 17 in number. The leaf stem, or petiole, is nearly as long as the leaf and flattened. Leaves of this species flutter and rustle in the breeze in much the same fashion as quaking aspen.

The flowers appear before the leaves in the spring, the long dangling worm-like catkins making this tree very conspicuous. Male and female flowers are on separate trees. The minute seeds, maturing in May and June, are contained in a small, hairy capsule and are widely dispersed by the wind. On freshly-burned areas where mineral soil is exposed, this species may seed heavily. Reproduction by root sprouting is also common when stimulated by fires or cutting of parent trees.

The most common and destructive insect on aspens is the forest tent caterpillar which occurs periodically in epidemic proportions, defoliating and occasionally killing areas of aspen and white birch. While the trees usually produce a second set of leaves the same year, repeated strippings may kill them, especially on wet sites. In heavily infested areas, the worms become so thick they may nearly cover the tree trunks. Woodborers often attack individual trees riddling the wood and making it of little value commercially. In forest stands, *Hypoxylon* canker is destructive to aspen of all ages; and the wood-decaying bracket fungus, *Fomes igniarius*, takes a major toll in merchantable wood volume.

Aspen forests, including both quaking and largetooth aspen, occur on nearly five million acres of Michigan's 19 million acres of timberland and make up 15 percent of the total cubic foot volume of timber in the state. Approximately 50 percent of the cubic foot volume lies in the north half of the Lower Peninsula, five percent in Upper Peninsuia. Unlike most other commercial species in Michigan, annual growth exceeds the drain. Growing shortages of other materials have created heavy demands on aspen for many purposes and its use is continuing to increase.

Commercially, largetooth and quaking aspen are not separated since the woods are nearly identical and have the same uses. The wood is light brown in color, often grayish, weak and uniform in texture. Though soft, it and other poplars are classed as hardwoods. It weighs 27 pounds per cubic foot in an air-dry condition. The principal uses are pulp for book and magazine papers, hardboard, lumber for boxes, pallets, crates and construction, matches, excelsior, food containers, furniture core stock, interior trim, toys, glued-up boards and unpainted furniture.

Identifying characteristics: Leaves alternate, oval, pointed, coarse toothed; leaf stems flattened; winter buds ½-inch long, dusty, lateral buds divergent; bark olive-green or brownish, smooth on young trees, furrowed near base on old trees.

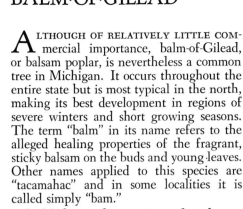

BALM-OF-GILEAD

Populus balsamifera L.

Although of relatively little commercial importance, balm-of-Gilead, or balsam poplar, is nevertheless a common tree in Michigan. It occurs throughout the entire state but is most typical in the north, making its best development in regions of severe winters and short growing seasons. The term "balm" in its name refers to the alleged healing properties of the fragrant, sticky balsam on the buds and young leaves. Other names applied to this species are "tacamahac" and in some localities it is called simply "bam."

In Michigan this species is found most commonly in the Upper Peninsula where it attains large size. It grows mostly on moist, alluvial soil in swamps, around lakes and along streams, and is commonly associated with swamp conifers, and with such hardwoods as red maple, white birch, aspen and black ash. Occasionally it grows in pure stands but is more often mixed with other species. Short-lived, balm-of-Gilead forms a good cover crop for spruce and balsam, gradually dying out and releasing these more valuable species.

Normally balm-of-Gilead grows to a height of 60 to 80 feet and a diameter of one to three feet. However, trees up to 100 feet high and six feet in diameter have occasionally been found. The crown is generally narrow and pointed, rather open, with slender, horizontal branches. It grows very rapidly, but is subject to decay at an early age and frequently becomes an unsightly tree with open cankers and warty bark. The shallow root system helps to spread this species by producing root suckers. It can be easily transplanted and propagated from cuttings, a fact which makes it valuable in shelterbelt plantings. Cuttings of more than one hundred native and foreign varieties of this and related species have been planted experimentally in Michigan and elsewhere in an effort to find the most rapid-growing trees for cellulose production. However, freezing, disease and damage by rodents have eliminated all but a few as possibilities for commercial use.

The bark on balm-of-Gilead twigs is reddish brown or dark orange in color, becoming greenish gray on the larger branches and upper trunk, and finally gray-black in color, thick and roughened by deep furrows and broad, flat ridges. Bark on young trees is fairly smooth, but warty bumps and branch scars soon mar the surface.

From a distance the foliage of this species has a slight rusty or bronze tinge due partly to the orange twigs and partly to rusty flecks on the backs of many of the leaves. The leaves are alternate, three to six inches long and about one-half as wide, rounded at the base, pointed at the end and finely toothed around the edge. They are shiny dark green above, whitish, or faintly rusty beneath, giving the tree a silvery appearance when the leaves are turned by the wind. The leaf stem is about 1½-inches long and is not flattened like the other native poplars. The young leaves are saturated with a fragrant wax or balsam used by bees in sealing their hives.

The flowers appear in April and May just before the leaves. As with the rest of the poplars, the male and female flowers are borne on separate trees, the male catkins three to four inches long and the female catkins four to five inches long. The fruit matures in May and June and is a capsule about ¼-inch in length containing minute, light-brown, hairy seeds, easily spread by the wind.

The terminal winter buds of balm-of-Gilead are very characteristic being nearly one inch long, slender and pointed, brown in color and covered with resinous, fragrant wax like the young leaves. The lateral buds are smaller and curved in toward the twig.

Balm-of-Gilead and cottonwood are frequently attacked by the poplar borer, a small worm which mines the limbs and trunks of small trees. Pinholes in the wood caused by the poplar timber beetle result in poor quality lumber and frequently provide entrance places for disease. The decay known as white heart rot, caused by *Fomes igniarius*, is common on balm-of-Gilead as well as the other poplars. The infected wood becomes soft and spongy.

As a forest type, balm-of-Gilead is not extensive or important enough to be classed by itself and is usually included with other broadleaved species under the general heading of swamp hardwoods. Likewise in lumber and pulpwood production statistics it does not appear alone but is included with figures for cottonwood and aspen. Estimates indicate that about five percent of the aspen lumber produced in the Lake States is balm-of-Gilead, and a similarly small amount is included as aspen pulpwood.

The heartwood is light reddish brown in color and the sapwood thick and white. It is soft, weak, easily worked, but warps badly and weighs only 23 pounds per cubic foot in an air-dry condition, making it the lightest of the commercial woods in Michigan. Its physical characteristics limit its uses to such things as shipping containers, excelsior, fruit basket veneers and pulp. A small amount is used for containers for druggists' supplies. It is not durable in exposed places, and rots quickly in contact with the soil.

Identifying characteristics: Leaves alternate, dark green above, pale or rusty beneath, finely toothed, pointed, rounded at base; leaf stem not flattened; foliage has bronze cast when seen from a distance; terminal winter buds one inch long, sharp pointed, resinous; bark dark orange and smooth on twigs, gray-black with flat ridges and furrows on old trunks.

COTTONWOOD

Populus deltoides Marsh.

COTTONWOOD IS THE MOST IMPORTANT of the poplars in the eastern United States, though not the most important in Michigan where it is now comparatively scarce as a commercial timber tree. At one time it was very common in the hardwood forests of the southern part of the state and was much used in farm construction because of the ease with which it could be handled and the long, clear boards it produced. Easily propagated from cuttings and rapid growing, it was often planted around homesteads and along roads for windbreaks and shade, and it is extensively used today in erosion control work and in shelterbelt plantings in the Great Plains region.

Cottonwood is rarely found north of the center of the Lower Peninsula except where it has been planted. It occurs naturally in rich, moist soils along river banks and in low lands growing with elm, soft maple, sycamore and basswood, but it also does well on much drier sites. An intolerant species, like other poplars, it is generally a dominant tree where it occurs and can frequently be spotted in farm woodlots towering above the forest canopy. Some of the largest trees in the state are cottonwoods.

Under forest conditions cottonwood develops a long, slender, cylindrical trunk, attaining heights up to 100 feet and diameters of three to five feet at maturity. Individuals, 150 feet in height and seven to eight feet in diameter, have been found west of the Mississippi River. Open-grown trees are generally tall, with massive trunks and spreading crowns. Branches are large, the lower horizontal, and the upper curving upward. The extensive, shallow root system makes this tree undesirable for city planting where roots may clog sewers and lift sidewalks and pavements. Many cities, in fact, prohibit the planting of this species for these reasons. Cottonwoods grow very rapidly, often increasing five feet in height and an inch in diameter in a year, but growth slows down after a few years, and trees begin to deteriorate at 70 to 80 years of age.

The bark on the twigs and young stems is smooth and yellow-green to brownish in color. Twigs frequently have ridges beneath the leaf scars. The bark on the older trunks is ash-gray and thick with straight deep furrows and broad rounded ridges.

Distinctive in shape, the leaves of cottonwood are triangular or "deltoid" in outline, three to six inches long and nearly as wide, with a broad, flat or slightly heart-shaped base, and coarsely-toothed margin. They are dark green and shiny above, pale beneath, thick and firm, and are arranged alternately on the twigs. The leaf stem is two to three inches long and flattened. When crushed the leaves have a sweet fragrance.

The flowers appear in long, densely-flowered catkins in April and May before the leaves develop. The male and female flowers are on separate trees. The seed-producing female catkins are six to eight inches or more in length by the time the seeds mature in May. The minute seeds are formed in capsules, are light brown in color and densely cottony, capable of being easily carried long distances by the wind. Approximately 350,000 seeds are required to weigh a pound. The abundance of these white, feathery seeds which shed from female trees is another reason why the cottonwood is not desirable as a city tree. Germination is generally high if wet soil is reached within a few hours after the seeds leave the tree, but few seedlings ultimately survive except in moist locations.

The terminal winter buds of cottonwood are ½- to ¾-inch long, sharp pointed, and covered with an aromatic resinous, brown, shiny coating. The lateral buds are somewhat smaller and point outward. Like the leaves, the buds have a pleasant odor when crushed.

Of the enemies of cottonwood, none is more serious than the cottonwood borer which causes damages and loss of trees in the Midwest. The adult insect is a beetle measuring nearly 1½-inches in length. When young, the beetles cut the bark preventing the flow of sap, and as adults they bore into the wood, weakening the tree and providing places for the entry of diseases. Carpenter ants and certain aphids also infest this species. Young cottonwoods, and frequently mature trees, are often attacked by the poplar canker causing the death of branches or a large portion of the crown.

Merchantable cottonwood timber in Michigan occurs most commonly as scattered individual trees in small farm woodlots, and from a commercial standpoint does not warrant special consideration.

The wood of cottonwood is soft and even-grained. The heartwood is brownish and the sapwood wide and white. It warps badly unless properly seasoned and has a sour odor when moist but no odor or taste when dry. A cubic foot of seasoned cottonwood weighs 28 pounds. The wood is used for boxes, crates, excelsior, food containers, furniture core stock, poultry coops and brooder houses, woodenware, bread and meat boards and butter pails.

―――

Identifying characteristics: Leaves alternate, triangular with flat or slightly heart-shaped base, coarse toothed, fragrant when crushed; leaf stem flattened; terminal winter buds ½- to ¾-inch long, resinous; small ridges below leaf scars on twigs; seeds minute, cottony; young bark yellow-green and smooth, becoming ash-gray with deep furrows.

BLACK WALNUT

Juglans nigra L.

Most valuable of michigan's hardwood timber trees, though it is one of our least abundant commercial species, black walnut occurs generally across the southern part of the state. It is most common in the extreme southwestern counties and is rarely found growing naturally above the Bay City-Muskegon line. Black walnut is one of six species of walnuts native to the United States and one of two species found in Michigan, the other being the somewhat less familiar butternut. Walnuts belong to the same botanical family as the hickories.

Prized for its excellent, durable wood, the once abundant black walnut was much used by the early settlers for rafters and beams in their houses and barns and also for fence posts. Many old southern Michigan farm houses built with walnut joists still stand.

The black walnut tree is not well adapted to extremes of temperature and moisture, and is very sensitive to soil conditions. Rapid growing, at least in early life, it makes its best growth on moist sandy loams and silt loams, commonly attaining heights of 60 to 80 feet and diameters of two to three feet. Greatest size is reached on the moist alluvial soils of the Ohio and Mississippi river valleys, where the trees have been known to grow 150 feet tall and six feet in diameter. Walnut normally occurs as an occasional tree associated with such species as white ash, black cherry, basswood, beech, silver maple, oaks and hickories. Very intolerant of shade, it is found always in a dominant position when in a dense forest stand. Its deep taproot makes transplanting difficult.

Walnut has been widely planted for shade as well as timber and nuts. Although a graceful and beautiful tree, in many respects it is not desirable as a lawn tree. Its leaves come late in the spring and are among the first to drop in the fall. The nuts clutter the lawn, and the husks contain a persistent yellow dye. The roots secrete a toxic substance known as "juglone" which is frequently damaging within a small radius to fruit trees and gardens.

In cross section a black walnut twig reveals a light brown or buff-colored chambered pith, in contrast to the dark brown chambered pith of the butternut. Bark on young black walnut twigs is light brown and hairy, becoming darker and smooth on older branches. On the trunks it is brown to black, frequently tinged with red, and often two to three inches thick with deep furrows and thin, rounded interlacing ridges. When shaved, the bark shows a rich chocolate-brown surface.

The terminal winter bud is about 1/3-inch long, ovoid and blunt. The buds are covered with fine, silky hairs. The lateral buds are similar but much smaller.

Walnut leaves are alternate, compound, one to two feet long, composed of 15 to 23 narrow, oval, pointed, finely-toothed leaflets 3- to 3½-inches long and less than half as wide, more or less opposite in their arrangement along the slightly woolly stem. They are distinctly aromatic when crushed. Bright yellowish-green on the upper surface, they are somewhat paler and covered with fine hairs on the under surface.

In April and May when the leaves are opening the flowers appear, both forms on the same tree. The staminate are in greenish drooping catkins on the previous year's growth and the pistillate in two- to five-flowered spikes on the new growth. In October the round fruits ripen, but frequently they remain on the tree until long after the leaves have fallen. Occurring singly or in clusters of two or three, the fruits are 1½- to 2-inches in daimeter with thick light yellow green husks that turn brown with age. The enclosed nut has a dark brown, hard, corrugated shell inside which is the oily, sweet kernel much used in cooking and flavoring. It is a favorite food of squirrels and many walnut trees have grown from nuts buried by these animals and forgotten. About 35 walnuts will weigh a pound.

Walnut is fairly free from serious insect pests and diseases when growing under forest conditions. Isolated trees and pure plantations, however, are often repeatedly defoliated by the "walnut datana" caterpillar which is undoubtedly the most serious and wide-spread pest of walnut, butternut, and hickories in Michigan. Leaf-spot diseases also may cause defoliation.

The sapwood of black walnut is whitish- to yellowish-brown and the valuable heartwood is chocolate or purplish-brown with a mild but characteristic odor. Strong, durable and coarse-grained, it is easily worked, checks and warps very little, and takes a high polish. A cubic foot of the seasoned wood weighs 38 pounds. It is used principally in the manufacture of fine furniture, cabinet making, interior finish both solid and veneer, and for gun stocks. Some of the most beautifully figured walnut for veneers comes from the swollen butt logs of trees cut off below the surface of the ground. Nearly all of the annual cut of walnut is shipped out of the state.

Identifying characteristics: Leaves alternate, compound, leaflets 15 to 23, finely toothed, aromatic; twigs with buff colored chambered pith; fruit nearly round, 1½- to 2-inches in diameter, often clinging after leaves drop; bark with interlacing rounded ridges, often red-tinged, cut surface chocolate-brown.

BUTTERNUT

Juglans cinerea L.

ONCE A HIGHLY RESPECTED TREE FOR ITS fine wood, its nuts, and its many pioneer uses, butternut, or white walnut, has gradually become a relatively uncommon, unheralded species. While individual specimens are still prized by their owners and the small annual nut crop jealously guarded, the species is of no commercial importance in this state. It is, however, a tree worth knowing.

Butternut extends as far south as northern Georgia and west to the Great Plains. In Michigan it is found scattered throughout the south part of the Lower Peninsula, and in Menominee and Delta counties in the Upper Peninsula. Nowhere common in this state, it is rare in its northern limits, becoming more frequent and of larger size in the extreme southern counties where it may be found in stands of basswood, elm, tulip, hickory, cherry, oak, and maple. Farther north its associates include yellow birch and white pine. It prefers deep, rich soils and river banks and ravines, but adapts itself to dry rocky soils as well.

In the forest butternut produces a tall, slender stem with a very narrow crown. Maximum sizes of forest-grown individuals measuring 100 feet in height and four feet in diameter have been found in the past. Usual sizes, however, are 30 to 50 feet tall and one to two feet in diameter. Where most commonly seen in fields and pastures, along fencerows and country roads, open-grown butternuts have wide, spreading crowns, with short trunks and horizontal lower branches, in general habit more stunted than walnut. The small branches are stiff and brittle, and old trees are often unsound, their ragged crowns filled with dead limbs. Very short-lived as trees go, butternuts seldom live over 100 years.

The stout twigs of butternut possess a chambered, chocolate-brown pith, and the bark is at first orange-brown to green in color, covered with a rusty, sticky fuzz. The bark later becomes gray-brown and smooth on branches and young trunks. Older trunks are ash-gray and distinguished by wide, shallow furrows, and narrow, smooth, interlacing, vertical ridges. The gray, ashy color of the tree is referred to in the botanical name *cinerea* from a Latin word meaning "ash." The inner bark of the roots possesses some medicinal value, and a sweet syrup was at one time boiled down from the sap.

The terminal winter buds are tapered and ½- to ¾-inch in length, brownish and fuzzy. The lateral buds are smaller, and located above a large, three-lobed leaf scar with a fuzzy upper margin.

Butternut leaves are alternate, pinnately compound, and 15 to 30 inches long with 11 to 17 stemless, thin leaflets, arranged oppositely along the stout, hairy stem. The leaflets are two to four inches long and one-half as wide, lance-shaped with somewhat flattened, parallel, finely toothed sides.

Yellow-green and wrinkled on the upper surface, they are pale and fuzzy beneath.

In May, along with the late-forming leaves, the small inconspicuous flowers appear, the male in thin, drooping catkins, three to five inches long, and the female in small, erect, clusters less than ½-inch long. In October the sweet, edible nuts mature, occurring singly or in clusters of two to five, often remaining after the leaves have fallen. They are two to three inches long and lemon-shaped, with a thin, soft, greenish brown sticky husk which readily stains the hands. An orange-yellow dye was once extracted from the husks and used to color homespun clothing. This use gave rise to the name "butternuts" for backwoods troops of the Civil War. Beneath the husk is a bone-hard, rough-shelled, four-ribbed nut containing the sweet, oily kernel from which the tree derives its name. Approximately 30 of the husked nuts will weigh one pound. At one time the nuts were plentiful on the fall markets, but are rarely found today.

The enemies of butternut are the same as those of walnut with the "walnut datana," a leaf-feeding caterpillar, the most common. In addition heavy winds and ice often break the brittle branches of this species providing entrance for fungi which cause the trees to rot inside at an early age, and often to die before reaching maturity.

As a lawn or street tree, the low-branching butternut has little to recommend it. It is not easily transplanted because of a deep taproot; it is not ordinarily symmetrical; its thin foliage, which opens late and falls early, is easily killed by frost; and the nuts litter the lawn and stain the sidewalks.

The wood of butternut is light brown in color with thin, lighter sapwood. Its satiny surface takes a high polish and grows darker and mellow with exposure. It is soft, weak, and coarse grained, easily worked, and, like walnut, does not warp or crack. A cubic foot of dry butternut weighs only 27 pounds.

This species is of little commercial importance today, although considerable quantities at one time reached the market often under the name of "white walnut." The branching habit of the tree produces beautifully figured wood. Because of its light color and weight it was used to panel the insides of carriages. It is still used today in expensive panel work, in cabinets and altars; and the current vogue for light colored furniture has increased its demand for fine custom pieces.

Identifying characteristics: Leaves alternate, compound, leaflets 11 to 17, finely toothed, sides somewhat parallel; twigs fuzzy, with dark brown chambered pith; upper margin of leaf scars fuzzy; fruit lemon-shaped, two to three inches long, husk green-brown, hairy, sticky; bark gray with wide, shallow furrows and smooth, interlacing ridges.

SHAGBARK HICKORY

Carya ovata (Mill.) K. Koch

RARELY FOUND NORTH OF THE BAY CITY-Muskegon line which divides the Lower Peninsula roughly into two halves, the shagbark hickory is a characteristic tree of dry wooded hills and fields in southern Michigan. Most important of the six or more species of hickory native to the state, the shagbark is one of nearly 20 species of hickory (including the pecan) native to North America. Many varieties and hybrids also are recognized, and the characteristics of even the common species are so variable as to make positive identification often difficult.

In Michigan the shagbark hickory is found mostly on dry, well drained, loamy sites, scattered in mixture with other hickories, oaks, white ash, walnut, black cherry and basswood. It occasionally reaches 80 feet in height and two or more feet in diameter. Best development, however, is attained on rich bottom land soils in southern United States where heights of 120 feet and diameters of more than three feet are reached. The slender trunk holds its taper well in to the typically oval or oblong, open crown which may be extremely small under crowded forest conditions.

The hickories in general are difficult to transplant, due to the strong, deep taproot they develop. The taproot of a young seedling may penetrate two to three feet the first year, while the top grows only a few inches. Though rugged and picturesque, the hickories do not make very desirable lawn and shade trees because of their slow growth and the litter of husks and nuts they drop every year.

The young twigs, at first brown and shiny, are marked with oblong lenticels and broad, heart-shaped leaf scars. In cross section the twigs show a star-shaped pith. Bark on older twigs and branches is gray, smooth and firm, while on the trunk it is broken into narrow, loose plates. These plates, frequently two to three feet long, are attached near the middle with the tips outcurving, giving the trunk an extremely ragged, shaggy appearance which, of course, gives the tree its common name.

Arranged alternately on the twigs, the dark yellow-green leaves are composed usually of five, and occasionally of seven, finely toothed leaflets that are broadest just above the middle and taper toward both ends. The terminal leaflet usually is the largest, being five to seven inches long and two to three inches wide, although the upper pair may be equally as large. When crushed, the foliage has a pleasingly pungent odor. A broad heart-shaped scar is left on the twig after the leaf drops off. Winter buds are ½- to ¾-inch long, dark brown and egg-shaped.

The flowers appear in May and early June after the leaves are nearly full grown. The staminate occur in drooping catkins four to five inches long, while the pistillate are two- to five-flowered spikes covered with fine, rusty hairs. Flowers of both sexes occur on the same tree. In October the rounded fruits appear singly or in pairs. One to 2½-inches in diameter, they are thick shelled, greenish-brown to brown when mature. The ¼- to ½-inch thick husk separates completely into four sections, exposing a four-ridged, oval, laterally compressed, brownish-white nut which has a sweet and edible kernel. This is the principal hickory nut of the market. Squirrels are very fond of this and other kinds of hickory nuts and are in a large measure responsible for the spread and regeneration of these trees. Between 80 and 90 shagbark hickory nuts, cleaned of outside husks, will weigh a pound.

While exceptionally free from diseases, save for some of the leaf-spotting parasites, hickory is very susceptible to many insects of economic importance. Particularly destructive is the hickory bark beetle, which may attain epidemic proportions and kill trees over large areas. Also extremely damaging are certain of the wood borers which reduce the quality of the wood for timber by boring fine holes deep into it and allowing stains and rots to enter. Certain grubs and weevils destroy the nuts and a defoliatng caterpillar known as the "walnut datana" may cause concern where shade or lawn trees are involved.

Hickory wood is one of the most specialized of our native woods. Its particular qualities make it almost irreplaceable for certain uses. The light brown wood combines strength, toughness, hardness and flexibility, characteristics not found combined in many other woods. Its dry weight is approximately 51 pounds to the cubic foot. Agricultural implements, handles, wagon stock, baskets and sporting equipment such as racquets and bows are made from it. It is finding increasing use as face veneer for paneling. As a fuel wood it is unexcelled; and meats cured in hickory smoke possess a distinctive flavor. In contact with the soil hickory is not durable, and it warps quite badly when exposed.

Identifying characteristics: Leaves alternate, compound, leaflets usually five in number, three upper ones large, nearly equal, broadest above the middle, tapering to both ends; winter buds brown, egg-shaped, large; husk, splitting completely into four parts; nut four-ridged, flattened, kernel sweet; bark gray with loosely attached outcurving strips.

PIGNUT HICKORIES

Carya glabra (Mill.) Sweet
Carya ovalis (Wang.) Sarg.

Among the most common and widely distributed of the Michigan hickories are the pignut hickories — the true pignut (*Carya glabra*), sometimes called "broom" hickory, and the oval or false pignut (*Carya ovalis*). Often these two species are not distinguished in botanical literature. They possess many of the same characteristics and are commonly confused, the chief differences being in the nuts.

The name "pignut" was probably applied to these species because the small, often bitter nuts were considered fit only for pigs. Actually the nuts are variable in taste, and as often as not may be sweet. The name "broom" hickory has been carried down from pioneer days when small hickory saplings were made into scrubbing brooms or brushes by cutting the flexible layers of sapwood into thin strips which were left fastened at one end, then bending them back beyond this end and tying them, leaving the heartwood core to be worked down to handle size.

The pignut hickories occur generally throughout the eastern United States and are typical components of the oak-hickory forest region. Best growth is attained on heavy clay and loam soils, but the trees are more commonly found on dry uplands and ridges, and in open pastures and fence rows. In Michigan these species occur as far north as Saginaw and Muskegon counties.

When growing under forest conditions these trees have narrow, round-topped crowns with ascending branches and relatively long clear trunks. Open grown trees, however, develop broad, rounded crowns with many drooping, contorted branches. Mature trees often measure 50 to 70 feet in height and one to two feet in diameter. Ages of 200 to 300 years are attained. Like the other hickories the pignuts possess deep taproots which make them difficult to transplant.

The tough twigs are much more slender than those of shagbark hickory. Greenish at first, they become reddish brown, smooth and shiny, with numerous pale, elongated breathing pores or lenticels. The bark is smooth and gray on young trunks, becoming dark gray or gray-brown on older trunks, and roughened by shallow furrows, with flat, interlacing, forking ridges. While it is usually tight, the bark occasionally separates into small, loose strips. It is hard but thin, and the trees are easily damaged by grass fires.

The leaves of pignut hickories are eight to 12 inches long, alternate, and compound, composed of five or seven leaflets, with the true pignut having mostly five leaflets, and the oval or false pignut more often with seven. Either species, however, may have leaves with both numbers of leaflets on the same tree. The stemless leaflets are arranged oppositely on the slender petiole, with the terminal leaflet the largest, and the basal pair of leaflets the smallest. They are widest near the middle, tapering toward both ends. The upper surface is dark yellow-green, and the under surface is lighter, with tufts of small hairs often in the angles of the veins. They have a pungent odor when crushed.

Pignut hickory buds are the smallest of the hickories, the terminal being ¼- to ½-inch long, with smaller laterals located just above the large leaf scars. They are dome-shaped and covered with shiny, reddish scales which frequently drop off in the fall or winter.

When the leaves are partly developed in the spring the flowers appear, the male on drooping stalks three to eight inches long in clusters of three, and the female in inconspicuous spikes about ¼-inch long. The inch-long fruits mature in October and are a valuable wildlife food. Those of the true pignut are usually egg-shaped or pear-shaped, with a thin husk which splits only part way to the base, enclosing a smooth, thick-shelled nut. The fruits of the false or oval pignut are oval in shape with a thin husk which splits in four segments clear to the base. The enclosed nut is four-ribbed above the middle, and thin-shelled. About 200 pignuts, cleaned of husks, will weigh a pound.

The most destructive enemy of these as well as other hickories is the hickory bark beetle, which mines the bark and growing tissue. The larvae working under the bark may completely girdle the tree. Adults feed in the buds and twigs in the summer and cause the premature falling of the leaves. Powder post beetles are particularly destructive to hickory lumber and other products such as handles. Diseases causing leaf spots are common but do not do serious damage.

The wood of the pignut hickories is similar to that of shagbark hickory but slightly heavier, weighing 52 pounds per cubic foot when air-dry, the heaviest of our native commercial woods. Like the other hickories it is hard, close grained, elastic and shock resistant. Its uses are the same as those of shagbark hickory. Because of its color appeal the wide white sapwood is preferred for most uses, although the reddish-brown heartwood possesses the same tough qualities.

Identifying characteristics: Leaves alternate, compound, leaflets five or seven, opposite, broadest near the middle, tapering to both ends; winter buds dome-shaped, ¼- to ½-inch long, with reddish-brown scales often dropping off in autumn; bark usually tight, with forking ridges; fruit of C. glabra pear-shaped, husk thin, opening only part way, nut unribbed, thick shelled; fruit of C. ovalis oval, husk thin, splitting in four segments to base, nut four-ribbed above middle, thin-shelled.

BITTERNUT HICKORY
Carya cordiformis (Wang.) K. Koch

Bitternut hickory bears the distinction of having the most extensive and most northerly range of any of the hickories. Often called "bitter pecan," this close relative of the true pecan is found from Maine and Quebec to Minnesota and south to eastern Texas and northern Florida. It is the most common hickory found in the northern prairie states. In Michigan it is reported to occur throughout the Lower Peninsula, but it is rare north of the Bay City-Muskegon line. In the southern part of the state, however, it is frequent, though not abundant, in stands of oak, soft maple, basswood, elm, and ash.

Bitternut hickory is a sturdy tree producing a tall, straight trunk and slender stiff branches under crowded forest conditions. In the open it develops a short trunk with many large ascending branches and a round-topped crown. Occasionally its form is distinctly elm-like with large arching branches and fine, drooping branchlets; and its leaves and bark resemble to some extent those of white ash.

The most rapid growing of all the hickories, it is also the shortest lived, seldom exceeding 200 years of age at maturity. Maximum sizes of 120 feet in height and four feet in diameter in the lower Ohio River bottom lands have been attained, but trees 50 to 75 feet tall with trunks one to two feet through are normal.

Its preference for loamy soils and wet sites has given this species the name of "swamp hickory" in certain localities; but it is adaptable to many soils and locations and is common in open fields and fencerows, as well as hardwood forests. It is tolerant of shade, and small trees may endure for many years under a heavy forest canopy, developing rapidly when the over-topping trees are cut, often forming small, pure groves. Like the other hickories it produces a deep taproot and is difficult to transplant.

The bark on the slender twigs is at first green and minutely hairy, becoming brownish on the small branches, and finally soft gray-brown to gray on the trunks. Smooth and unbroken on young trunks, it is hard and tight on old trunks, broken by shallow furrows and flat, close, interlacing ridges. Rarely if ever does it break into loose plates.

The leaves are alternate, compound, six to 10 inches long, and composed of seven to nine (occasionally five or 11) leaflets along a slender, hairy petiole. Stemless, except for the terminal one, the leaflets are lance-shaped, with the largest ones being from four to six inches long and 1- to 1½-inches wide, broadest at the middle. They are the smallest and slenderest of the hickory leaflets, and are more uniform in size than those of the other native species. Thin and firm with fine-toothed margins, they are bright, shiny green on the upper surface, paler and slightly downy below. They are pungently fragrant when crushed, and turn golden-yellow in the fall.

The terminal buds of the bitternut hickory are its most distinctive characteristic. Narrow and pointed they are one-half to three-quarters of an inch long, made up of two pairs of bright yellow bud scales with a granular surface. The lateral buds are smaller, somewhat four-angled, and often short-stalked.

In May or early June, after the leaves have formed, the flowers appear, both sexes on the same tree. The green stamen bearing flowers are in drooping, slightly hairy catkins, three to four inches long, on last year's twigs, several arising from the same base. The pistillate flowers are in short two- to five-flowered spikes about ½-inch long. The fruit, which occurs singly or in pairs, matures in October, and is a nearly round or slightly tapered nut, about one inch long, and coated with fine yellow hairs. The thin husk is ridged or winged above the middle, splitting only halfway to the base when it opens. The enclosed nut is reddish brown or gray-brown, pointed, smooth and thin-shelled, containing a bitter kernel. So bitter are these nuts that they are usually scorned by livestock and other animals, which probably accounts for the abundance of small bitternut hickory trees in our woodlots. An oil made from this nut was at one time used in the treatment of rheumatism. The nuts are slightly larger than those of pignut hickory, numbering approximately 150 to the pound.

The hickory bark beetle is undoubtedly the worst enemy of this as well as other hickories. Feeding under the bark the larvae of this beetle may kill the tree by girdling it, or may provide entrance for wood-rotting fungi. Many leaf feeding insects and leaf spotting diseases also attack this species. Its lumber, unless properly piled and seasoned, is frequently attacked by powderpost beetles which bore fine holes in it and reduce the inside to a labyrinth of powder filled tunnels.

The wood of bitternut hickory is inferior to that of shagbark, although it possesses many of the same qualities. Hard, tough and close grained, but not as strong or shock resistant, it is dark brown in color, with thick, lighter colored sapwood. It is very heavy, weighing 47 pounds per cubic foot when dry. The small amount reaching the sawmills is included with other hickories, and the wood is used for similar purposes, including such items as agricultural implements and tool handles.

Identifying characteristics: Leaves alternate, compound, leaflets usually seven to nine, slender, broadest at middle, tapering to both ends; winter buds ½- to ¾-inch long, slender, granular, bright yellow; husk winged above middle, opening only half way, nut smooth, kernel bitter; bark gray, tight with narrow flat, interlacing ridges.

IRONWOOD

Ostrya virginiana (Mill.) K. Koch

THE NAMES IRONWOOD AND HOP-HORN-beam are both descriptive of a small tree common throughout Michigan which has extremely strong wood and hop-like fruit. The strength of the wood of this tree is well known to woodsmen and farmers who use it for prying poles and levers. It was at one time, in fact, quite commonly known as "leverwood." This property of hardness and strength is recognized in the botanical name, *Ostrya,* which is from a Greek word meaning "a tree with hard wood."

A member of the birch family, our common ironwood is one of two species of *Ostrya* found in the United States, and is native throughout the area east of the Great Plains. The other species has one of the most restricted ranges of any tree in America, being found only in a few isolated spots in the Grand Canyon and in Utah.

In Michigan ironwood occurs as an understory tree scattered in hardwood stands, surviving even in the dense shade of hard maple, beech, birch, and oak, which are its common associates. Never very abundant, it is often considered a weed tree, seeding in following clear cutting of hardwood stands. It makes its best growth on well-drained, loamy soils, but is also common on dry, gravelly hills and in open, grazed woodlots.

Generally a slow-growing, small tree, ironwood seldom exceeds 35 or 40 feet in height and 12 inches in diameter, although trees 60 feet in height and two feet in diameter have been found in the past. When growing in crowded forest conditions it has a straight, slender, undivided trunk with an open crown composed of tough, slender branches and fine interlacing branchlets in gracefully drooping, horizontal sprays. In winter the delicate pattern of its leafless, zigzagging twigs is conspicuous among the coarse branches of surrounding trees. When growing in the open the trunk is short and the crown broad. The twigs are light brown in color with rounded or slightly pointed, chestnut-brown lateral buds about ¼-inch long and circular in cross section. There is no terminal bud. It is deep rooted and difficult to transplant.

One of the most distinguishing features of this tree is its thin, light gray-brown, shreddy bark made up of narrow, parallel, vertical strips which turn out at the ends. On small saplings the bark is not broken as it is on older trees, but is smooth and tight. The bark is rich in tannin, although it is not used commercially.

The leaves of ironwood resemble those of yellow birch. Arranged alternately on the twigs, they are 2½- to 5-inches long and approximately half as wide, taper pointed, and rounded or heart-shaped at the base. The margins are doubly toothed with fine, sharp points. They are smooth, dull yellow-green above, and somewhat paler beneath with tufts of fine hairs in the angles of the veins. Though firm and tough they are translucent even in faint sunlight. In the fall they turn a soft, clear yellow.

The flowers appear in the form of male and female catkins, both kinds on the same tree. The male or staminate catkins are formed in the late fall or early winter in drooping clusters of three or four at the ends of the twigs, and remain on the trees through the winter, providing along with the buds, one of the winter foods of ruffed grouse and bobwhite quail. In the spring, while the leaves are forming, the male catkins enlarge to nearly two inches long on the year-old twigs, and the smaller female or pistillate catkins develop at the ends of the new growth. The fruits mature in late August and September and are composed of several light green, flat, pointed, papery sacs arranged in cone-like clusters 1½- to 2-inches long resembling hops. The seeds are small flat nutlets about 1/3-inch long, which germinate the second year after planting. There are an average of 30,000 seeds per pound.

Ironwood has no serious enemies, but is attacked by the same pests which work on yellow birch and sugar maple. These include the spring and fall cankerworms, saddled prominent, and the forest tent caterpillar among the insects, while *Nectria* canker is the most common of the diseases.

The scattered occurrence and small size of ironwood make it commercially unimportant despite its many useful properties. Relatively little of it is made into lumber, and there are no special markets for it today. The wood is extremely hard, tough, and strong, and is very difficult to work. Weighing 50 pounds per cubic foot when dry, it is one of the heaviest of the Michigan woods, exceeded only by hickory. Physical tests show it to be 30 percent stronger than white oak and 46 percent more elastic. It is light reddish brown in color with thick white sapwood, and takes a high polish due to its close-grained structure. The wood is moderately durable in contact with the soil.

While the uses of ironwood today are confined to such things as handles, wedges, posts, flat car stakes and fuelwood, its uses in pioneer America were more extensive and included rake teeth, sled runners, ox yokes, kitchen utensils, furniture, wheel rims, spokes and axles, gear wheels, wagon tongues and whippletrees, and agricultural implements. The Indians used ironwood for bows.

Identifying characteristics: Leaves alternate, ovate, taper pointed, heart-shaped at base, doubly serrate, yellow-green, translucent; twigs fine, zigzagging, in flat, interlacing sprays; bark thin, light gray-brown, shreddy, with loose, narrow, vertical strips outcurved at the ends; fruit a hop-like cluster of light green, flat, papery sacs.

YELLOW BIRCH

Betula alleghaniensis Michx. f.

OF THE THREE SPECIES OF BIRCH NATIVE to Michigan, yellow birch or gray birch, as it is sometimes called, is the most important though not the most common. Typical of the hardwood forests of northeastern United States, southern Ontario, and Quebec, yellow birch has its greatest commercial stands in the Upper Peninsula of Michigan. Its beautiful wood is highly prized for furniture and veneer, and its prime logs bring the highest prices of any of northern Michigan's timber trees.

Rarely found in the southern part of the state, yellow birch attains its best development in the rich upland hardwood soils of northern Michigan where it grows with sugar maple, beech, hemlock, white pine, white spruce and balsam fir. Temperature seems to be an important factor in limiting its distribution. Not as tolerant as sugar maple, it will nevertheless survive years of almost complete suppression. Unfortunately, reproduction of this species even in well-managed stands is not very plentiful, and young seedlings are often heavily browsed by deer. Thus, the future supply is apt to be limited.

Yellow birch is one of the largest of our deciduous trees, often growing to 100 feet in height and four feet in diameter, attaining ages of 300 years or more. Trees of 60 to 80 feet in height and two to three feet in diameter are its normal, mature size, such dimensions being attained in 120 to 150 years. The open, rounded crown is composed of slender, more or less drooping branches. Under forest conditions, it develops a long, well-formed trunk. The root system is shallow and spreading. It is easily transplanted but not very satisfactory as an ornamental tree since its bark becomes gray and unattractive with age, and it does not thrive well in open situations.

The twigs are slightly aromatic with a wintergreen odor and taste, yielding oil of wintergreen on distillation. The bark on the twigs is smooth, silvery-gray, bronze or light orange in color with a satin-like sheen. On young trunks, it is silvery-yellow with elongated, horizontal markings, peeling around the trunk into fine, papery, curly shreds. Very inflammable, this thin bark is excellent for building camp fires even on rainy days, and it burns with a fragrant, oily smoke. The old bark becomes dull gray, ragged, breaking into large, thickened, irregular plates more or less curled or rolled back at one edge.

Three to five inches long, and half as wide, the leaves are alternate on the twigs, occurring singly or in pairs. They are oval in general outline, pointed at the tip and rounded or slightly heart-shaped at the base, and sharply double-toothed on the margin. The upper surface is dull, dark green and the under surface pale, yellowish green with fine, woolly tufts along the principal veins. The leaf stem is short, hairy and grooved. When crushed, the leaves are slightly aromatic.

The flowers appear in April before the leaves, usually both sexes on the same branch. The male catkins are two to three inches long, purplish yellow, slender and drooping. The female catkins are less than one inch long and erect. The seeds mature in autumn in small, conelike fruits. The scales of the fruit fall off, dispersing the small-winged seeds, but the slender core remains erect on the twig for some time. Approximately 400,000 seeds will weigh a pound. Large seed crops are produced at irregular intervals, and yellow birch seedlings spring up in almost any moist place such as in old stumps and on moss-covered rocks. Dense carpets of young seedlings are often formed after good seed years but competition is generally great, and few of them ultimately survive.

The lateral winter buds are approximately ¼-inch long, cone shaped and chestnut-brown in color, often on short spurs. There is no terminal bud.

Many defoliators and leaf-feeding insects infest yellow birch, but they rarely kill the trees and are important only because they retard growth. Certain diseases, however, do considerable damage to commercial timber by destroying the wood and eventually killing the trees. Among these are *Nectria* canker, and the tinder fungus, common on white birch.

Hard, heavy and very strong, the wood of yellow birch is highly prized where these special qualities are needed. It is close grained, light brown or reddish in color, with white sapwood, and takes a high polish. It is not durable when in contact with the soil. A cubic foot of air-dry yellow birch weighs 43 pounds. Its uses include furniture, veneer, paneling, flooring, door and sash trim, plywood, chemical distillation, charcoal, ties, brush handles, spools, shuttles, bobbins, musical instruments, and agricultural implements.

Identifying characteristics: Leaves alternate, three to five inches long, oval, doubly toothed, rounded or heart-shaped at base, faintly aromatic; terminal bud absent, lateral buds often on spurs; fruiting head erect; young bark silvery-yellow or bronze colored, peeling in thin, curly shreds; old bark gray with heavy curled plates.

WHITE BIRCH

Betula papyrifera Marsh.

WHITE BIRCH IS PROBABLY AS FAMILIAR a tree as any in Michigan. Its bark is unmistakable and is in striking contrast to the dark-colored barks and foliage of the pines, spruces, balsam and hardwoods with which it is associated. Often called paper birch and canoe birch, this is the species so frequently associated with the Indians who used its waterproof bark for canoes, wigwam coverings and utensils. Early settlers used the thin white sheets to write on.

White birch has a wide distribution extending throughout northern United States, Canada and Alaska. In Michigan it is found throughout the northern part of the state, and extends as far south as Ingham county. It makes its best growth in the rich, moist soil of swamps and river borders but is commonly found growing on fairly dry sandy sites with aspen, red maple, jack pine and oak. Like these species, it is intolerant and frequently seeds heavily or sprouts following fires where it may form small, nearly pure stands. Stump sprouting is very common, and graceful clusters, composed of many trunks, are seen almost as frequently as single trees, particularly in areas where fires have occurred.

Normally a small to medium-sized tree of 40 to 60 feet in height and 12 to 18 inches in diameter, it may grow considerably larger on certain sites. It is fast-growing but relatively short-lived, requiring only 60 to 80 years to reach maturity. Ordinarily trees only a foot in diameter are considered mature, and rot is common in trees of this size and even in much smaller ones. When young, the crowns are pyramidal in shape and composed of many slender, ascending branches. Old trees have open crowns with relatively few large branches and many fine branchlets. The root system is shallow.

The bark on the young branches is dull red to dark brown, becoming cream colored to chalky-white on the larger branches and trunks, and is marked by thin, horizontal lenticels or breathing pores. The base of the trunks of old trees is often nearly black. The thin, smooth bark is often unbroken on young trees, but on older trees may peel in fine shreds or in curled, papery strips or sheets. The inner bark is bright orange, turning deep red or brown when exposed. When once removed, the white outer bark is never renewed, and an ugly, dark scar is left. Deep cutting in the removal of bark may even kill the tree.

White birch leaves are firm, two to three inches long, and 1½- to 2-inches wide, alternate, and coarsely double-toothed. Ovate in outline, they are pointed at the tip and rounded or slightly heart-shaped at the base with short, smooth leaf stems dotted with tiny, dark glands. The upper surface is dark green, the under surface lighter green. In the autumn they turn clear yellow. They are not aromatic as are the leaves of yellow birch.

The flowers appear before the leaves in April and May, both sexes usually on the same branches. The staminate flowers are in pairs or clusters, three to four inches long, brown, slender and drooping; the pistillate flowers in small, green, cone-like heads, 1½ inches long, at first erect but later drooping. When the fruit is ripe in the autumn, these heads disintegrate rapidly, and the small, winged seeds are dispersed. About 700,000 seeds will weigh a pound.

The twigs do not have terminal winter buds. The lateral buds are narrow, ¼-inch long, and gummy. On old trees, they frequently grow on the ends of short spurs.

Use of white birch as an ornamental tree is discouraged in some localities because of the bronze birch borer which is the most serious insect pest that assails this tree. Presence of this insect is first noticed when tops of the trees begin to die. White birch leaves are one of the favorite foods of the forest tent caterpillar and are attacked by a host of other pests, including the birch leaf miner which produces a network of visible trails between the leaf surfaces. *Nectria* canker is the most serious disease of living white birch causing considerable commercial loss. Weakened or dead trees are rapidly destroyed by the "tinder fungus" which causes a white mottled rot in the wood.

White birch does not have the toughness or hardness of yellow birch and weighs five pounds less or 38 pounds per cubic foot when dry. However, it is strong and very close grained, with light brown heartwood and thick, white sapwood which often comprises most of the wood in rapidly-grown trees. It has excellent turning properties and is used for spools, bobbins, wooden ware, handles and dowels. Other uses include pulpwood, veneer, fuelwood, fireplace wood, shoe pegs, clothes pins, toothpicks, and novelties.

Identifying characteristics: Leaves alternate, two to three inches long, ovate, doubly toothed, rounded at base, not aromatic; terminal buds absent, lateral buds often on spurs; fruiting head drooping; young bark dark red or brown, older bark cream or chalk-white, peeling in thin shreds, papery strips, or sheets.

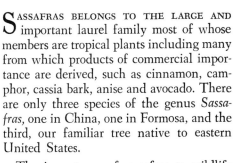

SASSAFRAS

Sassafras albidum (Nutt.) Nees

Sassafras belongs to the large and important laurel family most of whose members are tropical plants including many from which products of commercial importance are derived, such as cinnamon, camphor, cassia bark, anise and avocado. There are only three species of the genus *Sassafras*, one in China, one in Formosa, and the third, our familiar tree native to eastern United States.

The importance of sassafras to wildlife probably is greater than its timber value in this state for it produces dense thickets for cover, and its fruit is eaten by many birds and small animals. A sweet, pink tea, made by brewing the bark of the root, was used by the pioneers, and is still used to some extent today, as a spring tonic for "thinning the blood." Its alleged medicinal property made sassafras bark and roots much sought after by early explorers and it became one of colonial America's important exports. Shipments of sassafras were among the first cargoes sent to England from the Jamestown Colony by Captain John Smith.

In Michigan, sassafras is found chiefly in the southern agricultural area though it extends as far north as Crawford county.

Occurring generally on stony or sandy, well-drained soils, it will, however, grow almost any place except in swampy ground. It is common in fence-rows where it frequently grows in round-topped clusters. It is often regarded as a weed tree since it spreads into abandoned fields by means of root sprouts.

This species does not grow to a very large size in Michigan, and in fact when grown in the open often is not more than a large shrub. In forest stands, however, it may grow to much larger size, heights of 40 to 50 feet and diameters of 10 to 20 inches being not uncommon. In the South it may reach a diameter of five feet or more. The crown is generally narrow and open, composed of horizontal, brittle branches with up-curving twigs. It is a rapid-growing tree, difficult to transplant because of its fleshy roots, and not easy to propagate from seed. As an ornamental, its form is pleasing, and in the fall its brilliant orange, red and salmon pink leaves are unsurpassed in beauty.

The bark of sassafras twigs is smooth, shiny yellow-green, with a spicy odor and taste similar to that of the root bark. It becomes reddish on the branches and finally dark reddish brown on the trunk, with irregular, deep fissures and flat ridges. The bark used for making tea is taken from the roots lying near the surface of the ground.

One of this tree's most interesting features is its unusual leaves. They are alternate, three to six inches long, two to four inches wide, and variable in shape. They may be oval or may be composed of two or three finger-like lobes, all forms present on the same tree. The two-lobed form is the most curious because of its "mitten" shape. The leaf edges are smooth and the spaces between the lobes are rounded. Aromatic, thin and firm, they are dark green on the upper surface and pale beneath. The leaf stem is slender, about one inch long. A mucilaginous substance produced from the leaves is used in the South for flavoring gumbo soups.

The flowers appear in May along with the leaves, the staminate and pistillate on separate trees. Greenish-yellow in color, they are on slender stems in loose, drooping, few-flowered clusters. The berry-like fruit matures in September and October and is a round to oblong, shiny, dark blue berry about ¼-inch long, held by the base by the bright red, thick-stemmed calyx. There are about 5,000 cleaned seeds per pound. Sassafras fruit does not remain long on the tree for it is a favorite of many birds.

The winter buds are aromatic with the terminal approximately 1/3-inch long, oval and pointed, green and somewhat fuzzy. The lateral buds are much smaller.

Sassafras is practically free from damaging insects and diseases which is a point in favor of its more extensive use in ornamental plantings.

The wood is soft, weak, coarse-grained and brittle. It is slightly aromatic, orange-brown in color with thin yellowish sapwood. It shrinks less in drying than any other native hardwood. A cubic foot of air-dry wood weighs 31 pounds.

As a commercial wood, sassafras is unimportant although it has limited use in furniture manufacture, ties and fence posts. It is very durable in contact with the soil. Oil of sassafras is distilled from the bark and roots and is used in flavoring medicines, tobacco, root beer, gum, candy and soap. A small business is done each spring in the collection and sale of sassafras bark for tea. The principal supply of bark from which the oil is distilled comes from Virginia, Tennessee and Kentucky.

———

Identifying characteristics: Leaves alternate, aromatic, entire or with two to three finger-like lobes; twigs up-curving; fruit, a dark blue berry; buds, twigs and root bark aromatic; commonly grows in rounded, shrub-like clusters in fence rows on southern Michigan farms, and along roadsides.

SYCAMORE

Platanus occidentalis L.

DISTINGUISHED BY THE FACT THAT IT grows to a greater size than any other deciduous hardwood tree in North America, the sycamore or plane tree is an easily recognized, though relatively uncommon tree of southern Michigan. C. C. Deam, in his "Trees of Indiana," quotes early accounts of individual sycamores in the Ohio River valley, attesting the size. One tells of a hollow trunk in which one could "with perfect ease turn a 14-foot pole in the inside of the cavity;" and another describes a buttressed trunk "into whose hollow thirteen men rode on horseback . . . but there was room for two more." Sycamore is said to attain ages of 500 to 600 years.

Three species of sycamore are native to the United States, two in the West and one in the East, the eastern species being the only one that grows to a large size and is commercially important. The occurrence of this species in Michigan is largely confined to the south part of the Lower Peninsula, although it has been found as far north as Roscommon county.

Rapid growing, easily transplanted and not affected by dust or smoke, the native sycamore has been planted for many years as a street and ornamental tree. In recent years, however, the oriental plane and a cross between this and our native sycamore, known as London plane, have tended to displace the native species in landscape plantings because of their greater immunity to disease.

Sycamore is moisture-loving and intolerant of shade. It occurs as an occasional tree or in small clusters along streams and in rich, moist bottom lands, where it is associated with such trees as silver maple, elms, swamp oaks, willows and basswood. It may be found, however, on comparatively dry sites that have a moisture-holding subsoil.

While none of the old giant sycamores exists today, individuals 10 feet in diameter and more than 100 feet tall are found occasionally. Usual sizes of mature trees run from three to five feet in diameter and from 60 to 80 feet in height. Decay usually is present in the large trees and, thus weakened, they often are destroyed by high winds. The heavy, buttressed trunk frequently divides near the base into several secondary trunks. The branches in open-grown trees are heavy and spreading, with many zigzagging smaller branchlets, forming a broad, irregular crown. The root system is relatively shallow and spreading.

Most striking characteristic of the sycamore is the easily recognizable bark. Pale green or brownish and woolly on the small twigs, it becomes greenish or cream-colored and smooth on the large twigs and branches, occasionally with patches of dark green or brown. The bark on the trunks is a scaly, mottled mixture of varying shades of brown, green and cream, the result of a flaking off of the thin bark scales that exposes the suc-

cessively lighter layers beneath. Only at the base of very old trees is the bark roughened or fissured. In winter the light colored areas turn nearly white.

Sycamore leaves ordinarily are broader than long. They are among the largest of the simple native tree leaves, frequently being 10 inches wide. Arranged alternately on the twigs, they have three to five broad pointed lobes having slightly toothed or wavy margins and shallow indentations. The leaf stem is two to three inches long, with a hollow base beneath which the pointed winter bud forms. The leaves are thin and firm, bright green above and paler beneath, and turn russet brown in the autumn. The terminal winter bud is absent; the lateral buds are about ¼-inch long, shiny, pale brown, conical and blunt.

The drooping, dense round clusters of minute flowers appear in May at the same time as the leaves, both staminate and pistillate on the same tree. In October the dangling brown balls of seeds, about an inch in diameter, ripen. They remain on the trees most of the winter, gradually scattering the fine seeds in the wind. From 100,000 to 170,000 seeds weigh a pound. These seeds are so extremely delicate that only five to 10 percent have strength to germinate, and they must have ideal moisture conditions to survive.

Most serious and widespread of the pests attacking sycamore is an anthracnose disease, caused by a fungus, which may defoliate the trees and "kill back" the twigs for many years in succession. This seldom kills the trees, but because of it they lose vigor and often become dead-topped and deformed. A leaf-sucking insect known as the "lace bug" is also common.

Sycamore wood is very pleasing and distinctive in appearance, being light reddish-brown in color, with conspicuous rays appearing as short, closely-spaced lines. It is even-textured, coarse-grained, with interlocking fibers, moderately heavy (36 pounds per cubic foot, dry weight), hard, and difficult to split. It is the butcher's first choice for a meat block. Unfortunately, it warps easily when sawed into lumber and is difficult to work. The wood is used also in making boxes, barrels, drawers, furniture, interior trim, handles and woodenware. It rots quickly in contact with the soil. In Michigan the annual cut is very small. Largest commercial production of this species is in Mississippi and Louisiana.

———

Identifying characteristics: Leaves alternate; lobes, three to five, wide-based, pointed; end of leaf stem hollow; seeds clustered in hanging balls which persist through winter; bark pale green or cream-colored, mottled by darker scaly patches of older bark.

BEECH

Fagus grandifolia Ehrh.

ONE OF THE MOST DISTINCT AND EASILY recognized of our native trees, the beech is of considerable importance in Michigan from the standpoints of aesthetics and wildlife as well as timber. Beechnuts are a valuable and favored food for squirrels, raccoons, pheasants, grouse, bear, deer and many other birds and animals. A beautiful tree providing dense shade, beech is highly prized as a landscape and park species, although in such situations its smooth gray bark is often disfigured by initials and other carvings which remain for the life of the tree.

Beech is typical of the hardwood forests of the eastern part of the United States. It occurs throughout the Lower Peninsula of Michigan and in the Upper Peninsula as far west as Iron County where it gradually drops out of the stands. Its common associates are hard maple, yellow birch, basswood, white ash, elm and oak. In northern Michigan it is one of the chief components of the "maple-beech-yellow birch" forest type. One of the most tolerant of our hardwoods, its young seedlings will survive years of suppression in dense shade. Deep, rich, well-drained loams produce the best growth, but beech will thrive on a variety of soils provided there is ample moisture.

When growing under forest conditions, beech is a tall, slender tree with a continuous central stem, short horizontal branches and a narrow crown; but it produces an unusually short, thick trunk and a broad, heavy crown of spreading branches when grown in the open. Under forest conditions, beech reaches a height of 80 to 100 feet and a diameter of two to three feet at maturity. It is slow growing and may attain an age of 300 to 400 years. Easily damaged by fire, old trees and even comparatively young ones are frequently hollow as a result. The root system is shallow and spreading except for a deep tap root. Root sprouts are common and are the origin, rather than seeds, of some of the beech reproduction.

Beech is easily recognizable from a distance because of the steel- or ash-gray color of its bark and its smooth surface which is not roughened or furrowed with age. It may become mottled with light and dark blotches or bands, and frequently contains old branch scars. It is thin and easily scarred. The twigs are shiny olive-green, and have a zigzag appearance.

Firm and leathery, the leaves of beech are three to six inches long and about one-half as wide, oblong, pointed at the tip and wedge-shaped at the base. A straight vein terminates in each of the sharp, incurved teeth around the margin. The leaves are shiny, dark green above and light yellow-green beneath. The leaf stem is very short. In the fall the leaves turn to light gold or buff and may persist through most of the winter.

The flowers and leaves appear at the same time in April and May, both flower sexes on the same tree. The male or staminate flowers are in round heads an inch in diameter on long, drooping stems; the female or pistillate flowers in clusters of two to four on short stems. The fruit matures in the autumn and is a stiff, spiny, four-valved burr which often clings to the tree after the nuts are gone. The nuts are triangular, ¾-inch long, brown shelled, the meat sweet and edible. There are usually two, but occasionally three, in each burr. Approximately 1,500 seeds will weigh a pound. Good seed crops occur only once in every three to four years and often the nuts may be abundant but contain little or no meat.

The terminal winter bud of beech is nearly an inch long, slender, sharp pointed, reddish brown in color and shiny. The lateral buds are similar in shape and size.

Beech has few serious insect pests although it is often attacked by certain maple caterpillars where maple and beech occur in the same stand. Among the diseases, beech is more subject than any other Michigan tree to the white heart rot caused by the "false tinder fungus." This together with a yellow sapwood rot do considerable damage to commercial timber trees causing the wood to become punky and the butts of large trees hollow.

Seasoned beech wood weighs 43 pounds per cubic foot, is hard, tough, strong and closed grained. The sapwood is thin and whitish, the heartwood light red. Beech wood is easily recognized by its color and by the rays which appear as evenly spaced, short, dark lines. Its principal uses are for flooring, brush and tool handles, coat hangers, food barrels and boxes, agricultural containers, furniture, charcoal, and chemical distillation. It makes excellent fuelwood.

———

Identifying characteristics: Leaves alternate, shiny green, pointed, straight veined, sharp toothed, short stemmed; fruit a four-valved burr; nuts triangular, sweet; buds shiny, slender, sharp pointed, one inch long; bark steel-gray, smooth.

SMALL TREES

As a group, the native small trees occupy unique and important places in our forests and landscapes. Many people who pay little attention to large trees are aware of these small members because of their flowers and fruits or their interesting shapes, which can be closely observed and enjoyed.

Many of the small trees are "understory" trees, occupying the space mid-way between the low forest vegetation and the forest canopy, and capable of growing in dense shade. Some are considered "pioneer" species because they are often the first to revegetate forest areas opened by fires or logging, or to creep into idle farmlands. Others, with their introduced relatives and cultivated varieties, are basic to the landscape industry. Some are often shrub-like; some are valuable to wildlife; some are of interest to herbalists; and some may become plain nuisances to farmers and forest managers. But all are a part of our rich and varied flora, and need no other excuse for existing than to add beauty and interest to woodlands, parks, roadsides and homesites.

In most cases the wood of the small trees is of little interest. Exceptions are dogwood which has a long history of use, blue beech and hawthorn because of their extreme strength, and juneberry because it is one of the heaviest of our native woods.

The next several pages are devoted to these small and frequently colorful components of our tree resource.

ONE OF THE MOST EASILY RECOGNIZED of our understory trees, blue beech is interesting in all seasons with its smooth, sinewy looking bark, its clusters of seed bracts hanging like miniature Chinese lanterns, its delicate, translucent leaves, and beautiful autumn coloring. It is a member of the birch family, and like its close relative, *Ostrya virginiana*, is also called "ironwood" and "hornbeam," allusions to the toughness of its wood. Another name, "musclewood," is not a reference to its strength, but rather to the unique appearance of the trunk. Of the 26 species if the genus *Carpinus* found throughout the world, blue beech is the only one on this continent, where it is typical of hardwood forests of eastern United States and Canada. It is common in southern lower Michigan but rare in the northern Lower Peninsula and Upper Peninsula.

While blue beech prefers deep, rich, moist soil, it grows on a variety of sites, and is very tolerant of the heavy shade of the overtopping forest canopy. It is slow-growing and seldom attains a height of more than 30 feet, but the diameter of the trunk may reach 18 to 20 inches. The crown is generally low, rounded and thin, with irregular branches and delicate branchlets, casting light shade. It is attractive and interesting as an ornamental, but is not easily transplanted.

Blue beech bark is smooth in texture, much like that of our native beech. This, together with its slate-gray color gives rise to its preferred common name. The fluted, muscular looking contours of the surface, with vertical or interlacing ridges of lighter color give the trunk a streaked appearance, and provide an immediate means of identification. The winter buds are brown, about ⅛ inch long, with white margined scales in four rows making them squarish in cross-section.

The leaves are alternate, two to five inches long and about half as wide, with a tapering point, parallel veins, and finely doubled-toothed margins. They are light green and thin, turning orange to brilliant red in the fall.

The separate male and female flower catkins appear in April or May, and the tiny brown, nutlike seeds mature in midsummer attached to three-pointed, leafy bracts which hang in clusters three to six inches long, often remaining into the winter. The seeds are eaten by squirrels and many birds, including grouse, quail, pheasants and wild turkeys.

Blue beech wood is light brown in color, with thick whitish sapwood. It is extremely hard, tough and heavy, weighing 49 pounds per cubic foot. Its small size gives it no commercial value, but its toughness made it useful in earlier times for tool handles, levers and ox yokes.

Identifying characteristics: Leaves alternate, taper-pointed, double-toothed; twigs fine; seeds in hanging clusters of three-pointed bracts; bark blue-gray, smooth, muscular looking.

Female flower spike

Male flower spike

ALTHOUGH ONLY ONE SPECIES OF MUL-berry, the red mulberry (*Morus rubra*), is indigenous to the eastern United States, the introduced white mulberry (*M. alba*), and especially its variety the Russian mulberry (*M. alba. var. tatarica*), are the ones most frequently seen. The arrival of white mulberry, a native of China, predates the American Revolution, having been imported from England in a futile effort to establish a silk industry in this country. It is presently found mostly in the East and South. Russian mulberry, a more hardy variety, was introduced about 1875 by Mennonites, and has been widely planted as an ornamental and for shelterbelts and farm windbreaks. Locally its range has been extended by birds, and it is now more or less naturalized.

Native red mulberry is an infrequent tree in Michigan today, and, in fact, is considered by many botanists to be "rare" and deserving of special protection. Its natural habitats are deep woods and river bottomlands in the southern third of the Lower Peninsula. Russian mulberry, on the other hand, is commonly found in landscape plantings, and as an "escape" from cultivation along roadsides and fencerows throughout the southern half of the Lower Peninsula.

Mulberries are small to medium sized trees which attain heights of 30 to 60 feet or more, with short trunks 10 to 30 inches in diameter. Often there are multiple stems supporting branchy, spreading, dense, round-topped crowns. They are used in certain kinds of landscape plantings, but are considered messy when growing near sidewalks and streets because of the abundance of soft, staining fruits which mature and drop over a period of several weeks.

Mulberry bark is greenish tan to reddish brown on the branches and trunks, with shallow furrows showing lighter color in the grooves. Very old trunks are deeply furrowed. Winter buds are about ¼ inch long, light brown and dome-shaped.

Leaves are alternate, three to five inches long and about as wide. They are coarsely toothed, and may be unlobed or have two to five lobes. The upper surface is dark green, and ranges from shiny to dull. Leaf stems and twigs exude a milky juice when cut.

The flowers are unisexual, appearing in May and early June in spikes one to two inches long, male and female on the same or different trees. The blackberry-like fruit ripens from July to August, changing from pink to deep purple. Sweet, juicy and edible, they are sometimes used for pies and jellies, and can be made into a cooling drink. They are favorites of birds and squirrels.

Identifying characteristics: Leaves alternate, with coarse teeth, unlobed or with two to five lobes; fruit purple, blackberrylike; bark greenish tan to red-brown.

A CURIOUS SMALL TREE, WITH LARGE tropical-looking leaves and a banana-like fruit, the paw paw looks out of place in Michigan. And it should. It is a member of the custard apple family of mostly tropical plants. Of six North American species, this is the only one which grows to tree size and which reaches as far north as Michigan. "Custard apple" and "wild banana" are other names which aptly describe this interesting understory tree with its soft edible fruit, so well known to Indians, early explorers and settlers. It still occasionally appears in marketplaces in the South.

Paw paw is most common and makes its best growth in the Ohio and Mississippi valleys. It is on the northern limits of its range in Michigan where it occurs in scattered locations in the southern third of the Lower Peninsula, most frequently in the southwestern counties. Capable of growing 20 to 30 feet tall with a diameter of six to eight inches, it is more often much

shorter in this locality. It prefers rich, moist soils and forest shade. Shoots readily form from the roots and it often forms dense thickets. As an oranamental it offers variety and interest.

The bark is thin, brown-gray with dark gray blotches, and smooth except for small wart-like bumps. It has a disagreeable odor when bruised. The inner bark is fibrous and was used by Indians to make fabric, ropes and fish nets. Winter buds are very small and covered with dark rusty brown fuzz.

The leaves are the largest simple leaves of any of our native trees, measuring 6 to 11 inches long and about half as wide. They are alternate, toothless, broadly lance-shaped, tapering to both ends, and clustered near the ends of the stout twigs. They turn deep yellow in the fall.

The exotic looking, reddish purple flowers appear in May and June with the leaves. They are nearly two inches across, composed of six petals, and posses an un-

pleasant odor. The fleshy fruits, looking somewhat like stubby bananas, are generally ripe in October, having changed from light green to purple to nearly black in color, and from smooth to prune-like in texture. They are three to five inches long, appearing singly or in clusters of two or three. A single fruit may weigh a half pound. They have a sweet, spicy fragrance, and contain a soft edible pulp which is custard-like in both color and consistency, with a mild, sweet, fruity flavor. Several large seeds about the size of lima beans are enclosed. In earlier days paw paws were used in jellies, or eaten raw. They are favorites of opossums, raccoons, squirrels and foxes.

Identifying characteristics: Leaves alternate, large, toothless, tapered; flowers large, magenta, with rank odor; fruit fleshy, stubby, green to purple, with sweet yellow pulp; bark gray.

The MOUNTAIN ASHES ARE ATTRACTIVE small trees, which put on a showy floral display in late spring and early summer, and in the fall flash their bright red berries against contrasting green foliage. They are not true ashes, but are members of the rose family, with nearly 80 species and varieties, mostly European and Asian. Three species are native to North America, including one western shrub, and two eastern species which commonly attain tree size. Both eastern species (*S. americana,* and *S. decora*) are native to Michigan. The tree most commonly seen in landscape and street plantings, however, is the European mountain ash or Rowan tree (*S. aucuparia*). No attempt will be made to distinguish between these various species here, since they closely resemble one another.

The eastern mountain ashes are north-country trees, natives of northeastern United States and Canada as far north as Hudson Bay. In Michigan both species are found primarily in the Upper Peninsula, with occasional appearances in the northern Lower Peninsula as far south as Missaukee and Roscommon counties where browsing deer keep them cropped to low shrubs. They grow best in rich, moist soils of river banks and swamp borders, and in rocky forest areas. They normally reach only 15 to 25 feet in height and six to eight inches in diameter, with slender trunks supporting rounded or pointed crowns. They are often shrublike in the wild.

The bark is smooth, variable in color, ranging from light reddish brown to gray-brown, with conspicuous lenticels. The inner bark is fragrant. Winter buds are about ½ inch long, dark red, with a curved tip and sticky surface (woolly in the European species).

The leaves are alternate, compound, six to nine inches long, with 9 to 17 lance-shaped, finely toothed leaflets, which turn yellow in the fall. In May or June, after the leaves have grown, the creamy white, fragrant flowers appear in showy clusters, three to five inches across. The individual five-petalled flowers are only about ⅛ inch wide. The brilliant fruits mature in September and October, hanging in heavy clusters which often remain on the trees through the winter. The orange to red berries are round, about ¼ inch in diameter, and very bitter. They attract many songbirds, and are especially favored by cedar waxwings and grouse. Indians and early settlers made a tea from the berries which was used to treat scurvy, the juices providing rich doses of vitamin "C". A brew made from the bark was administered for nausea and heart disease.

Identifying characteristics: Leaves alternate, compound, leaflets finely toothed; flowers white, in broad, dense clusters; fruit orange to red berries; bark smooth, red-brown to gray-brown.

AMONG MICHIGAN'S TREES, LARGE AND small, none provides a more welcome sight in early spring than juneberry with its blossoms announcing the end of winter. The profusion of white flowers look from a distance like wisps of smoke against the browns and grays of still sleeping forests and hillsides. Several members of this complex genus of the rose family are shrubs, but this species commonly attains tree size with a single stem. Besides the name juneberry, it is known equally well in some parts of the country as "service-berry," "sarvis," shadbush," and "shad-blow." The "shad" part of the name, common in the East, tied the early spring flowering to the spawning runs of shad fish.

Juneberry is found extensively in the central and northeastern parts of the United States, and throughout Michigan, growing on a variety of sites and soils ranging from rich, upland forest areas to sandy pine plains. It is common as an understory tree, but makes its best growth on forest edges and in the open, where it is most apt to be multi-stemmed. Normally a small tree 15 to 30 feet tall, with trunks four to six inches in diameter, it may grow to 60 feet in height and a foot in diameter. It has a thin, irregular crown of fine branches.

The bark is light reddish brown to gray, and is smooth on young trees; on older trees it is slightly scaly, streaked by shallow, dark colored vertical grooves. The winter buds are ¼ to ½ inch long, with large reddish brown scales, and a sharp, tapered point.

Juneberry leaves are alternate, oval, three to four inches long and about half as wide, rounded or slightly heart-shaped at the base. They are dark green above, pale and smooth beneath, with sharply fine-toothed margins. (A very similar species found in northern Michigan, the "downy serviceberry," *A. arborea*, has wooly leaf stems and underside veins.)

In April or early May, before the leaves or as they are unfolding, the dainty white flowers appear in erect or drooping clusters. The five narrow, strap-like petals are nearly an inch long and wide-spreading. The round fruits, ripening from June to August, turn from bright red to dark purple, with a slight bloom. They are juicy and sweet, and make excellent jams and jellies, and can be used like blueberries in pies and muffins, or dried like currents or raisins. Many kinds of birds and animals devour the berries. Bears sometimes break the trees down in their eagerness to reach them.

The wood of juneberry is one of the heaviest of our native woods, equal to shagbark hickory in weight at 52 pounds per cubic foot.

Identifying characteristics: Leaves alternate, oval, margins fine-toothed; flowers with five narrow petals, appearing before or with the leaves; fruits round, purple, sweet; bark smooth.

Long after many of the other trees have leafed out and flowered in the spring, the wild crab suddenly brings forth its contribution to the beauty of the season. It is well worth waiting for, for the delicate shell-pink, fragrant blossoms, partially hidden among the leaves and thorny branches, are a joy to discover. A member of the rose family, and closely related to our domestic apples, this small tree is widely planted as an ornamental, as are its numerous cultivated varieties and forms. The trunk is sometimes used as stock for grafting cultivated apples. Other names for the wild species are "crab apple," "American crab," "garland tree," and "wild sweet crab," although the last must refer to the fragrance of the blossoms, not the fruit, which is anything but sweet.

A native of northeastern North America, wild crab is found in Michigan only in the southern half of the Lower Peninsula where it inhabits rich moist woodlands and stream banks, as well as pastures, fields and fence-rows. As an understory tree in the crowded woods it may have a straight, slender stem 15 to 25 feet tall and six to eight inches in diameter; but when growing in the open it is a many branched tree with a rounded crown and stiff, contorted limbs. Its thornlike branchlets provide a protected nesting place for songbirds.

The bark on the twigs and small branches is gray and smooth, turning reddish brown on the trunk, and broken by thin vertical curls. The winter buds are pointed, ⅛ to ¼ inch long, and bright red.

The alternate, slender-stemmed leaves are bright green, two to three inches long and nearly as wide. They are sharp pointed, deeply toothed, frequently with two large lobes above the rounded base.

The flowers appear in May, after the leaves. Pink at first, they gradually turn to white in full bloom, with a faint blush of pink remaining. They are perfect, five-petalled, showy, 1 to 1½ inches across, in five-to six-flowered clusters, and they fill the air with a spicy, wild fragrance. The small, round, hard apples are fully grown in September, often hanging on their long threadlike stems through the winter. They are 1 to 1½ inches in diameter, pale green, with a waxy, almost oily, surface. The flesh is tempting to sample, but is very tart, sweetening in storage. Pioneers made cider from them, and they were, and still are, used to make tangy, orange-red jellies and preserves. The fruits of this species and many of the cultivated crabs are relished by many kinds of birds and animals, including grosbeaks, pheasants, raccoons, foxes and deer.

Identifying characteristics: Leaves alternate, sharp-pointed, deeply toothed; branchlets small, thornlike; flowers pale pink, fragrant; fruit green, waxy, on slender stems; bark red-brown, scaly and curly.

Prunus americana Marsh.
Prunus nigra Ait.

ONE OF THE MOST PLEASING OF OUR small native trees is wild plum, which bursts in a profusion of white flowers piling like snow on bare branches in early spring. Attractive in its own right as an ornamental, wild plum is the basis for many horticultural varieties cultivated for both flowers and fruit. It is barely distinguishable from the more northern species, Canada plum, and since their ranges overlap in Michigan, they are often treated together as "wild plum."

Never abundant, wild plum has an irregular range including much of eastern United States and extending as far west as Wyoming and Utah. In Michigan it is found only occasionally in the northern part of the state, but it is locally abundant in the southern part where it is most likely to be discovered growing in thickets on river banks, in fence-rows, and on the borders of country roads. It prefers rich soils, but grows on a variety of sites. It is a small tree, usually 15 to 30 feet tall with a distorted trunk, 6 to 12 inches in diameter, which divides a few feet above the ground into stout, angular, thorny branches, forming a narrow or spreading crown. It sprouts freely from the roots, and its formidable thickets offer fine protection for birds and small animals which also enjoy the fruit.

The bark is reddish brown to purple on young branches and trunks, dotted with lenticels, and armed with thornlike spurs, one to two inches long. On older branches and trunks it becomes gray and shaggy with curly-edged plates. The winter buds are about ⅛ inch long, dome shaped and chestnut brown.

The leaves are alternate, broadly lance shaped, three to five inches long, with sharp points and short petioles. The margins are finely double-toothed. They are dull green, thick and firm, with a coarse surface.

The heavy floral display appears in May or early June before the leaves. Long stemmed and pungently fragrant, the five-petaled white flowers are about an inch across, grouped in clusters of three to five, the numerous, long stamens giving them a fuzzy look. The plums ripen in August and September and quickly fall from the trees. They are nearly round, 1 to 1½ inches in diameter, and range in color from peach to orange-red to dark red, often with a slight bloom or coating. Beneath the thick skin is a yellow, sour but edible flesh, much prized in earlier times for jellies and preserves. The fruits were also used as a laxative, and Indians gargled an extract of the inner bark for sores of the mouth and throat.

Identifying characteristics: Leaves alternate, lance-shaped, margins double-toothed; flowers white, clustered, appearing before leaves; fruit orange-red to dark red; twigs with thornlike spurs.

Pin cherry, or fire cherry, is a typical "pioneer" species, invading openings created by logging, forest fires, and farm abandonment. It is short lived, serving as a nurse tree in the ecological succession of forests, giving way to more permanent species of conifers and hardwoods. It is attractive to wildlife, particularly birds, and in fact is called "bird cherry" in some localities. A member of the rose family, its clusters of small white flowers and brilliant red fruits on long pinlike stems make it a pleasing part of the northern forest scene.

Pin cherry ranges from northeastern North America as far west as British Columbia and the eastern slopes of the Rockies, inhabiting mostly light sandy soils and rocky hillsides. In Michigan it is a common companion of aspen and jack pine in the north, occurring only occasionally in the southern half of the Lower Peninsula. It grows rapidly, attaining a height of 20 to 30 feet or more, and a trunk diameter of 6 to 10 inches. It is single stemmed, with a narrow, open, usually pointed crown, of slender, straight branches. It spreads by both seeds and root suckers, and often forms dense thickets. It is considered a nuisance in many localities.

The bark on the twigs is smooth, lustrous red, marked with orange lenticels. It becomes deep red on the older branches and trunks, with conspicuous horizontal rows of lenticels, peeling near the base into thin, papery curls. It is bitter but pleasingly fragrant. The winter buds are rather blunt, about ⅛ inch long, with a cluster appearing at the tip of each twig.

The alternate leaves are narrow, two to five inches long and taper pointed, with undulating sides, and margins of fine incurved teeth, as in black cherry. They are bright green and shiny on the upper surface, and paler beneath, turning red in the fall. They are attacked by many insects including the cherry leaf bettle and the eastern tent caterpillar.

The white, five-petalled, perfect flowers are about ½ inch across, on long pinlike stems, occurring in round topped clusters of five to seven. They appear in May and June with the leaves. The fruit develops in July and August as light red, long stemmed, miniature globes, about ¼ inch in diameter. They are tart but tasty, and are relished more by birds and small animals than by humans whose consumption is largely confined to jellies. At one time it was used in cough mixtures. The long stems of the flowers and fruit immediately distinguish this species from the black and choke cherries.

———

Identifying characteristics: Leaves alternate, narrow, with fine, in-curved teeth; flowers and fruit on long, pinlike stems; bark with pleasant odor.

THE SMALL CHOKE CHERRY IS ONE OF the most widely distributed trees in North America, ranging from the Arctic Circle to Mexico, and from the Atlantic to British Columbia. It is found throughout Michigan, where it is common on cutover and burned-over timberlands, abandoned farms, fence-rows and roadsides. Choke cherry is well named, for its tiny fruits are extremely bitter. It is one of our abundantly flowering wild trees, its dense spikes of white blossoms looking like rolls of intricate lacework.

Choke cherry may grow to a height of 25 to 30 feet and a diameter of six to eight inches, but normally it is smaller, and may be shrub-like in appearance with several leaning or crooked stems. Its seeds are spread by birds, and it also reproduces by root suckers to form dense thickets. The crown may be narrow or spreading.

The bark on the twigs and young stems is reddish brown and shiny, becoming gray-brown on the larger branches and trunks, and remaining smooth or only slightly fissured. Twigs and stems are dotted with light colored lenticels. The bark has a rank odor when peeled or crushed. The light brown winter buds are ¼ to ½ inch long and taper pointed.

The leaves are alternate, two to four inches long, about one-half as wide, the widest part above the middle. They are abruptly pointed. The margins have fine, sharp serrations like saw teeth. This feature helps to distinguish choke cherry from black cherry and pin cherry which have incurved leaf margin teeth. The leaves are dark green above, pale and hairless beneath.

The white flowers appear from May to early June after the leaves, but earlier than those of black cherry which they resemble. They are clustered along a central axis in densely flowered spikes, four to six inches long. The individual flowers are short-stemmed, perfect, ¼ to ½ inch across, and five-petaled like other members of the rose family. The fragrance is not pleasing. The tiny fruits appear from mid-July to September, changing in color from yellow to red to deep lustrous purple. The flower calyx is absent, a feature which distinguishes this species from black cherry. They are very tart, but make good jellies. They are sought by many species of song birds, and by pheasants, grouse, wild turkeys, raccoons, deer and bears.

Choke cherry root bark was once brewed by the Indians to produce a bitter remedy for colds, stomach ailments, and fever. Peach and cherry orchardists usually eradicate this species near their orchards since it attracts certain disease carrying leafhoppers. It is also highly susceptible to "black knot" disease, and to nest building caterpillars.

Identifying characteristics: Leaves alternate, widest above middle, with fine, saw tooth margins; flowers and fruit in long spikes; flower calyx absent from fruit; bark with rank odor.

THE HAWTHORNS ARE AN EXTREMELY complex group of small trees and shrubs, with 1000 wild species, varieties and forms described, most of which are North American. Many botanists feel, however, that there are actually relatively few pure species. Most of those which attain tree form and size are found in northern United States. References point to over 40 species throughout Michigan, including trees and shrubs.

Hawthorns, also called "thornapples," or just "thorns," are members of the rose family and are horticultural favorites, widely planted for landscape and garden purposes because of their compact form, attractiveness to birds, and the beauty of their flowers, summer and autumn foliage, and fruit. In the wild, hawthorns are equally attractive, although often considered a nuisance in pastures and woodlots.

Found on a variety of sites and soils, the sun-loving hawthorns are most frequent in open woods and pastures, and along roadsides and streambanks. They often form dense thickets valuable for wildlife protection and food. Although some species are found in nearly all parts of the state, they are most abundant in kind and numbers in the southern farm area.

The arborescent forms are usually low and spreading, seldom exceeding 25 feet in height, with symmetrical round or flat-topped crowns, often broader than high. Branches are angular, horizontal or upsweeping; branchlets zig-zagging and armed with slender, stiff thorns.

The bark varies from tan to gray to dark red. Twigs and small branches are smooth, while the trunk is finely textured with shallow grooves and thin, narrow plates or scales. Winter buds are small, rounded, and shiny brown.

The small alternate leaves vary greatly in size and shape between species. The margins are singly or doubly serrated, sometimes deeply lobed.

Usually white, or occasionally pinkish, the conspicuous five-petalled, perfect flowers appear in May and June, with or after the leaves, in rounded or flat-topped clusters. They are not pleasantly fragrant. By October the small round fruits are mature, often remaining through the winter. They may be scarlet, deep red or purple, or a blend of red and yellow. The flesh ranges from dry and mealy to succulent and edible. They are relished by quail, partridge, pheasants, grouse, rabbits and deer. For humans, they have been used to treat high blood pressure and insomnia.

The physical qualities of hawthorn wood are referred to in the name *Crataegus*, the Greek word for strength.

Identifying characteristics: Leaves alternate, variable, single-or double-toothed, often lobed; twigs thorny; flowers white, five-petaled; fruits small, round, mostly red.

No SPRING IN SOUTHERN MICHIGAN would be complete without the gorgeous displays of redbud. As a landscape tree and in its native woodland haunts its magenta pink freshness causes heads to turn and smiles to form. It has long been a favorite of horticulturists because of its ease of planting, rapid growth, pleasing form and ability to flower when only four or five years old. It graces small homes and estates with equal charm. Both George Washington and Thomas Jefferson made references in their writings to the planting of redbuds and flowering dogwoods in their gardens. The name "Judas tree," sometimes applied to our American species, has its source in an old European legend holding that this was the tree from which Judas hanged himself, and that the formerly white flowers were foreverafter red in shame.

Redbud grows naturally in most of the eastern United States. Michigan is on the northern fringe of its range, and it is found wild principally in the extreme southern counties, but seldom above the Huron-Clinton and Grand River valleys. As an understory tree, it inhabits rich wooded bottomlands and stream borders, where its striking color is heightened by the dark backdrop of the forest. Fortunately it will grow on many sites, a fact which enhances its landscape value. Whereas redbud may grow to 50 feet in height in the South, here it usually grows to only 15 to 30 feet with a trunk diameter of 8 to 12 inches. It usually divides near the ground into a broad, rounded crown of straggly branches.

The bark on young branches is shiny brown with fine grooves, turning gray-brown and scaly with interlacing ridges on older branches and trunks. The winter buds are about ⅛ inch long, dome-shaped, and reddish brown.

The leaves are alternate, broadly heart-shaped, two to six inches long, and dark shiny green. They turn yellow in the fall. In April or early May before the leaves emerge, the ½ inch long reddish purple, long-stemmed flowers appear, arranged in clusters of four to eight, crowded along the bare stems. The base of the flower, or calyx, is a deeper color than the orchid-shaped petals revealing a two-toned combination upon close inspection. The fruits mature in late summer and often remain on the branches through the winter. They are dry pods, characteristic of the legume family, two to three inches long, tapered at both ends, and containing 10 to 12 flattened seeds. They have no significant wildlife value.

Identifying characteristics: Leaves alternate, broadly heart-shaped; flowers small, reddish purple, in crowded clusters, appearing before leaves; fruits are dry pods, often remaining through winter.

Acer spicatum Lam.

Two small maples are frequent components of the understory in our northern hardwood forests and are often found within a few feet of each other. One of these is mountain maple, easily recognized by its large leaves, and usually reddish leaf stems and twigs. Its common associates are beech, maple, yellow birch, white pine and hemlock, and its small companion in the under-growth, the striped maple. It is common throughout the northern Lake States and in the mountains of the northeastern states, extending in the Appalachians as far south as North Carolina and Tennessee. In Michigan it is reported throughout the state, but it is rare in the south half of the Lower Peninsula. It has been observed in Oakland and Lapeer Counties. Its large leaves and small size make it an interesting landscape tree.

Mountain maple normally grows to only 20 to 30 feet in height and four to eight inches in diameter. Under the dense shade of overtopping trees, it develops a crown of small branches pointing upward as if reaching for the light. Often there are several stems in a cluster, giving it a shrub-like appearance.

The bark on the twigs is reddish to green and velvety hairy. It becomes reddish brown to gray on older trees. Indians used a decoction made from the bark of the trunk and roots to treat eye infections, dysentery, asthma and heart trouble. The tree has no particular wildlife value, although the young twigs and bark are browsed by deer. Winter buds are bright red, fuzzy, ⅛ to ¼ inch long, dome-shaped or flattened.

As in all maples, the leaves and twigs are opposite each other. The leaves are four to six inches long and about as wide, with three prominent, blunt, lobes, and occasionally two smaller lobes toward the base. The margins are made up of coarse, pointed teeth. The petioles are long, mostly red, with an enlarged base. The upper leaf surface is a dull, bright green, the lower is lighter and slightly downy. They add to the brilliance of autumn in the hardwoods with their colors of orange and scarlet.

The small yellow-green flowers appear in June after the leaves are full grown, usually with separate male and female flowers which both occur on the same floral spike. The spikes are upright, four to six inches long, and conspicuous, hence the botanical species name, *"spicatum."* The fruits are small paired samaras, with wings about ½ inch long, and with a visible cavity on one side of each head. They are bright red at first, turning to brown in late autumn. They hang in long clusters which often remain after the leaves are gone.

Identifying characteristics: Leaves opposite, large, with three blunt lobes, margins coarse-toothed; flowers in long, upright spikes; seeds in pairs, winged, in hanging clusters.

Acer pensylvanicum L.

STRIPED MAPLE IS ONE OF TWO SMALL members of the maple family represented in Michigan, and, like its companion mountain maple, is a denizen of the shady northern hardwood forests. Known also as "moose maple," "moosewood," "whistlewood," and "goosefoot maple," it can be quickly identified by its unique striped bark and large goose-foot shaped leaves. It is very abundant in some areas, thriving in the dense shade of the beech-birch-maple-hemlock forest, where it sometimes forms the principal undergrowth. It ranges from the mountains of New England, west to Minnesota, and south in the Appalachians to Georgia. In Michigan it is found in the northern third of the Lower Peninsula, and in the Upper Peninsula as far west as Houghton County.

Striped maple is a slender, open-crowned tree, or shrub-like cluster, often with a wavy trunk. It normally attains heights of 15 to 30 feet and diameters of four to eight inches; but specimens over 50 feet tall and more than a foot in diameter occur in the Huron Mountains in northern Marquette County. It prefers the rocky or moist sandy soils found along stream banks and in the deep woods.

The distinctive bark is olive green or reddish and smooth on the twigs, becoming light reddish brown or tan with green stripes on the branches and trunks, which may be slightly furrowed. The tender, sweet bark of the twigs and young stems is heavily browsed by deer and moose. In the spring the bark slips easily from the sap-filled twigs providing a hollow tube for making a whistle, hence one of the early names of this tree, "whistlewood." The terminal winter buds are about ½ inch long and pointed, sitting on short stalks. The bud scales are keeled, bright red, and smooth.

The leaves are opposite, five to seven inches long and equally as wide, with three taper-pointed lobes, and double-toothed margins. The bases are rounded or heart-shaped, and the petioles short. Bright green in the spring and summer, they turn yellow-gold in the fall. The tiny yellow flowers appear in May and June, after the leaves, the male and female in separate, drooping clusters, four to six inches long. The seeds are paired samaras with spreading wings about ¾ inch long. They grow in long, hanging clusters which mature in the fall and remain long after the leaves have dropped. Each seed head has a cavity on one side.

———

Identifying characteristics: Leaves opposite, large, with three taper-pointed lobes, margins double-toothed; flowers in long drooping clusters, seeds in pairs in hanging clusters; bark green, or tan striped with green.

WELL KNOWN FOR THEIR ORNAMENTAL virtues and extensively planted for both flowers and fruits, the viburnums number over 100 species throughout the world, of which some 20 are native to North America, 10 being found in Michigan. While they are mostly shrubs, the nannyberry is the principal exception to this, ranging from a shrubby form to a true tree in size. It is a member of the honeysuckle family, and is closely related to the elders whose large flower clusters are similar in appearance. Other names by which it is sometimes known are "sheepberry" and "wild raisin," although the latter is actually a separate species.

Nannyberry is common in northeastern United States, and occurs throughout Michigan, though it is scarce in the Upper Peninsula. It is generally found where the soil is rich and moist, along the borders of swamps, marshes and streams, at forest edges and roadsides. It will also do well on much drier sites, and is tolerant of city conditions. These qualities lead to its frequent use as a landscape plant. Under forest conditions it may grow to 25 or 30 feet in height with a single trunk 6 to 10 inches in diameter, and a narrow or spreading crown.

The bark is green to reddish brown on the twigs, with a somewhat fuzzy and granular surface. Branches and trunks are sepia brown, with the surface broken into small ridges or scaly plates. The winter buds of the leaves are reddish, ½ inch long, and slender; the flower buds are longer, swollen at the base, with a tapering point, and they are completely covered by two scales.

Leaves are opposite, ovate, two to four inches long and about half as wide, with a long, slender, tapering point. They are bright green, firm, with sharply toothed margins, and a grooved or winged petiole.

In May or June, after the leaves, the creamy white flowers appear in showy, round-topped clusters, three to five inches wide. The individual flowers are perfect, about ¼ inch across, with the yellow tipped stamens protruding like pins in a pin cushion. The fruits ripen in September, hanging in loose clusters on red stems. They are dark blue when ripe, with a slight bloom, and are sweet and edible. They look like raisins when dried. Many kinds of birds and animals are known to eat the fruits including song birds, pheasants, grouse, squirrels, foxes, skunks, raccoons, rabbits and deer. Sheep and goats and other livestock also find them appetizing.

Identifying characteristics: Leaves opposite, taper-pointed, margins sharp-toothed; flowers white, in dense, round-topped heads; fruit dark blue, in loose clusters.

F LOWERING DOGWOOD IS CONSIDERED BY many to be our most decorative tree. In any season it graces woodlands, roadsides, parks, and homes with its unique shapes and variety of seasonal offerings. Its flat floral displays on upsweeping branches suggest oriental flower arrangements.

Dogwood has a long history of use. It was a favorite in landscape plantings in colonial parks and estates. Indians and early settlers made a bitter brew of its bark and flowers to treat malaria, jaundice and cholera; and the same extract substituted for quinine during the Civil War. These ingredients are still available in herb stores. Its tough wood has long been used for shuttles and bobbins in the textile industry.

Found throughout most of eastern United States, flowering dogwood ranges across the southern third of the Lower Peninsula of Michigan. It is most abundant in the southwestern counties, extending as far north as Muskegon County. It prefers rich, moist soils and shade, but will grow on relatively dry sites and in the open. It is a small to medium sized tree, 20 to 40 feet in height with a trunk diameter of 5 to 12 inches. Its slender spreading branches with upturned tips form a flat or rounded crown.

The bark is light brown to reddish brown, and deeply checkered in an alligator-hide pattern. The root bark yields a scarlet dye used by Indians to color feathers and porcupine quills. The conspicuous winter flower buds are gray, dome-shaped, four sided and stalked. Leaf buds are small and inconspicuous.

Dogwood leaves occur opposite one another, and are clustered at the ends of the twigs. They are three to six inches long, about half as wide, tapering to both ends, with curved veins paralleling the smooth margins. Bright green in summer, they turn to purple and scarlet in the fall. In May and early June the flat clusters of flowers appear along with the leaves. Four white, notched, petal-like bracts form the showy display, and surround the small cluster of greenish yellow true flowers in the center. Bunches of small, oval fruits ripen in October and continue the colorful display with their shiny, scarlet coats. They are bitter, but relished by birds, squirrels, and deer, and are one of the preferred foods of wild turkeys.

The wood of flowering dogwood is brownish in color, strong, extremely tough and heavy, second only to hickory in weight at 51 pounds per cubic foot. In addition to its use for shuttles and bobbins, its toughness also made it useful in earlier days for tool handles, wedges, wheel hubs, hay forks and rake teeth; and in more modern times for golf club heads.

Identifying characteristics: Leaves opposite, tapering, veins parallel, curved, margins smooth; flowers with four notched white bracts around green-yellow center; fruit scarlet; bark checkered.

Tulip poplar

Basswood

Catalpa

Oak catkins

Black locust

Jack pine—male flowers with pollen cloud

Sugar maple—male flowers

ABOUT TREE FLOWERS . . . . .

Flowers are a part of all trees, large and small. Some are conspicuous and showy, and some are minute and seldom noticed by the casual observer. Some are perfect, with both male and female parts in the same blossom; and others are unisexual, with the pollen-bearing and seed-producing organs in separate flowers, sometimes on separate trees. Floral characteristics are the principal feaures used to group trees into families. The flowers shown on this page are representative of some of the larger trees, in contrast to the small trees on the preceding pages.

Jack pine—female flower head

. . . . . AND WINTER BUDS

Tree buds (and leaf scars) are as varied as flowers, fruits and leaves, and can be used as winter identification. Buds are formed in mid-summer when tree growth ceases. Some are opposite one another along the twigs, some alternate, some are terminal, some are large, and some are nearly hidden. They contain the embryonic leaves or flowers packed beneath protective scales, ready to endure the winter, and carrying the promise of another spring.

Beech

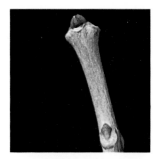

White ash

Silver maple

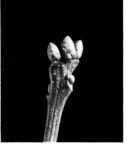

White oak

White birch

Butternut

Basswood

FOREST SUCCESSION

A Northern Michigan Case History

ONE HUNDRED YEARS of change in the forests of northern Michigan are represented in the three-part painting on the following pages by wildlife artist Charles Schafer. The stumps and the flames and the furrows in the upper left part of the picture tell of the forest's rebirth—the first stages of its development. Logging harvested Michigan's virgin forests, and repeated fires and attempts to farm kept new trees from invading much of the open land. After cultivation was abandoned, and fire protection started, the land began to grow weeds, grass, shrubs, and trees. The following thirty years, as depicted in the lower left, was a period of healing and growing, resulting in the establishment of a new forest. This first forest was temporary and gradually gave way to the more stable forest, shown on the right side of the picture, which ultimately occupied the area.

Whenever land and its plant cover is disturbed and then left alone, it responds to that disturbance in a systematic and predictable manner. This orderly process of plants re-establishing themselves is called plant succession. Just as the succession of plants is predictable, so also is the succession of wildlife associated with each plant phase. Plant succession provides the base on which a program of forest and game management can be built.

The first phase in succession is the growth of the plants that require much sunlight and cannot grow in shade. They include annual grasses and low-growing herbs and woody shrubs. Following this is a group of plants which are the larger semi-shade tolerant shrubs and intolerant trees. The sun-loving plants associated with the first stage are gradually shaded out by the taller plants and trees which develop into a dense young forest toward the end of stage two. These are the trees that make up the earliest forest stands after fires and abandoned farming, and which will temporarily dominate the area. Most are fast growing and short-lived (about 60 years), and become established over extensive areas about the same time, forming an even-aged forest. They include, typically, the aspens, white birch, and jack pine. Associated with these will be found red maple and scrub oak.

It is the changing condition of plants gradually developing from grass and brush country into a young forest that provides the greatest diversity of ground cover. It produces many desirable kinds of plant foods and supports the greatest variety of wildlife in the greatest abundance. Wildlife species present will range from the prairie chicken and sharp-tailed grouse in the scattered open grassland areas to snowshoe hares, deer, ruffed grouse and coyotes in the young forest.

Most of Michigan forests were at this diversified phase of plant succession from the late 1920's to the 1940's. It was at this time that deer numbers reached their maximum. The highly productive habitat resulted after logging and wild fires had occurred over a wide area in Michigan during the late 1800's and the early years of the present century. Effective fire control allowed this stage of succession to continue. It permitted re-establishment of a pulpwood industry and in the process created optimum deer habitat. The large number of deer produced during this stage of growth in Michigan was a phenomenon that may never happen again.

The young forest, or stage two in plant succession, changes rapidly. Entire landscapes are altered in the natural process of forest development, going from grass and brush to a young forest in 15 to 30 years. In this relatively short period, prairie chickens reach their peak in abundance and decline rapidly. Snowshoe hares, ruffed grouse and deer numbers "peak" a short time later. However, the animals, particularly deer, will be in trouble before the end of this stage because of the shading out of desirable food and cover plants, and over-browsing of edible parts of shrubs and small trees.

Today, much of Michigan's forest land is entering a third stage, the final or "climax" phase in the process of plant succession. Low-growing trees and shrubs are disappearing. They are being replaced by tolerant trees which are able to regenerate themselves and grow under the shade of large parent trees. Among these are some of our most valuable timber trees — white pine, yellow birch and sugar maple. The "climax forest" is made up of trees of many ages, and will perpetuate itself unless altered by logging, fire, or wind.

Once trees which do not require sunlight in the early stages of their growth reach maturity, they form a dense shade which will reduce the amount and quality of cover and food for the wildlife that lived in earlier stages of the succession. The wildlife found in this forest is limited, including such arboreal species as squirrels, porcupines, martens, and fishers, and a variety of small birds like the pileated woodpecker heard tapping on a hollow tree.

Thus, undisturbed, the forest progresses through a gradual and predictable series of changes from bare ground to its ultimate tree composition. Likewise, the wildlife changes at each stage, with a rapid build-up to high populations followed by a gradual decline to a lower, stable level.

By proper forest management man can arrest this natural succession, holding the forest in an intermediate stage, or recycling it, thus providing, not the maximum of either wildlife or forest products, but a lower and sustained level of both.

Michigan Department of Natural Resources

The plow followed the axe in much of northern Michigan, but unproductive land was soon abandoned. It started to heal, however, through the invasion of grasses and low-growing shrubs. This prairie stage was home to the prairie chicken.

The grasses and shrubs provide the seed bed for sun-loving trees which finally create a dense, even-aged, pulpwood forest. This transition stage in forest succession supports the greatest variety and abundance of wildlife.

As succession continues, sun-loving trees are replaced by those which will grow in shade. This climax forest produces our most valuable trees. Its wildlife is limited until harvesting creates openings and starts low vegetation again.

53

WHEN AUTUMN COMES

While it has long been held that frost, in the whimsical guise of Jack Frost, brings about the annual glorious fall color display, the phenomenon is in reality the result of complex chemical processes, not related to frost, which take place in the trees during their preparation for winter.

During the spring and summer the leaves have served as factories, manufacturing food necessary for the tree's growth. This process, known as "photosynthesis", is carried on in the leaf cells by green chlorophyll bodies which give the leaves their green color. The food is made, in the presence of sunlight, by combining carbon from the air with hydrogen, oxygen, and various minerals supplied in the water which the roots absorb from the soil. In the fall when cool weather brings a slowing down of the vital processes, the work of the leaves comes to an end. The machinery of the leaf factory is dismantled, so to speak, and the green chlorophyll disintegrates.

With the breakdown of the chlorophyll the characteristic colors of the different species begin to emerge. The variation, even within a single species or on a single tree, depends upon the kinds, amounts and mixtures of various chemical substances already present or newly formed in the leaves. *Xanthophyll* is responsible for the clear yellow of aspen, birch, tulip poplar, ginkgo and hickory; *carotene*

produces the gold, orange and red of some of the maples; the formation of *anthocyanin* in certain species results in the pink, scarlet and purple hues of black gum, dogwood, sassafras, white oak, ash and red maple; and the presence of *tannin* is linked to the tan, russet and brown of beech and oak.

While the leaf is changing, other preparations are being made. At the point where the stem of the leaf is attached to the twig, a special layer of cells begins to develop which slowly blocks the flow of water to and from the leaf, and gradually severs the connecting tissues. When the leaf finally falls, the place where it had been attached is marked by a characteristic "leaf scar," varying in shape with each tree species.

Fallen leaves contain relatively large amounts of valuable elements, such as nitrogen and phosphorus, which were originally in the soil. Decomposition of the leaves enriches the top layers of soil by returning these elements, and at the same time provides for an accumulation of water-absorbing, insulating humus. If fires are allowed to burn this surface, the most valuable of the fertilizing elements are changed by the heat into gases and escape into the air, and the protective humus may be destroyed.

AMERICAN CHESTNUT

Castanea dentata (Marsh.) Borkh.

A CENTURY AGO AMERICAN CHEST-nut was one of the most common and valuable of the hardwoods in the eastern United States where it was abundant in many forests, particularly in the mountainous areas. Its wood found its way into a variety of products, its sweet nuts filled the markets every autumn, and it was prized for its beauty as an ornamental tree. Today, because of an imported disease, this species has been practically eliminated throughout its range, and old-growth chestnut trees are now a rarity.

Never very abundant in Michigan, the natural range of chestnut in this state is confined to the southeastern part extending only as far north as St. Clair County. It has been planted elsewhere, however, and specimens which have escaped the disease can still be seen today in many localities as far north as the Grand Traverse area. It thrives on a variety of soils and sites from sandy loams to dry rocky pastures and hillsides.

In crowded forest stands chestnut is a dominant tree, developing a long, clear trunk often with a diameter of three to four feet and a total height of 80 feet at maturity. Maximum sizes, found in the southern Allegheny Mountains, were 10 feet in diameter and 120 feet high. When grown in the open this species usually has a broad, rounded or pyramid-shaped crown with a short, thick trunk and heavy branches spreading out near the ground. Oftentimes the spread of the tree exceeds the height. Chestnut is one of the fastest growing and longest lived of our hardwoods but it is difficult to transplant since it usually produces a deep taproot.

The twigs and sprouts are chestnut-brown to dark purplish brown in color and dotted with small, whitish lenticels. The bark on old trunks is hard and thick, grayish brown in color with moderately deep furrows and flattened, often continuous ridges. It is rich in tannin.

The dense foliage is made up of simple, drooping, thin leaves, six to eight inches long and two to three inches wide, arranged alternately on the twigs. They are oval or oblong in outline and tapered at each end, with a leaf stem about one inch long. The veins are parallel, each terminating in a coarse, sharp-pointed tooth on the margin of the leaf. Yellow-green and shiny on the upper surface, they are lighter colored and dull on the underside. In the fall they turn a golden-yellow. The winter buds are chestnut-brown in color, ⅛- to ¼-inch long, egg-shaped, with two or three visible scales. There is no terminal bud.

In June and July, long after the leaves have fully developed and other trees have flowered, the chestnut bursts into bloom. There are two kinds of flower heads. One is creamy-yellow and showy, made up of small, mildly fragrant staminate flowers densely clustered along a slender, erect, pencil-like stalk, six to eight inches long. The other is a slightly shorter, inconspicuous stalk, containing green pistillate flowers at the base, and scattered staminate flowers along the upper part.

The burs develop rapidly and are nearly full grown by mid-August, ripening in the fall and opening after the first frosts. Tan-colored when mature, they are round, 1½- to 2½-inches in diameter, and composed of a dense covering of stiff, branched prickles on a woody husk which splits into four sections. Inside, in a bed of soft velvety down, are one to three reddish- or chestnut-brown nuts. Usually flattened on one or two sides, the nuts are one-half to one inch across, top-shaped, and covered with soft fuzz near the pointed end. They will vary from 100 to 150 per pound. The kernel inside is sweet and edible either fresh or roasted.

While certain insects attack chestnut, their damage is over-shadowed by the chestnut blight disease. One interesting insect, however, is the chestnut timber worm which bores into both living and dead trees producing wood which is cut into lumber and marketed as "wormy chestnut." The chestnut blight, *Endothia parasitica,* which has brought the American chestnut to the point of extinction, kills the tree by attacking and destroying the inner bark. The disease was introduced from Asia shortly after 1900, prior to plant quarantine laws, on infected nursery stock of Asiatic chestnuts. It was first noticed in 1906 on native trees in the New York Zoological Park where some of the stock had been planted. From there as well as from other points it spread rapidly and in 25 years had covered almost the entire range of chestnut. No effective means of control exists, and no resistant strains have been found.

The wood of chestnut is soft, coarse grained, porous and weak, and weighs only 28 pounds per cubic foot when dry. It is a pale reddish brown with lighter colored sapwood, and has a characteristic minute, shiny fleck in the open pores. It is one of the most durable woods in contact with the soil or above the ground. Chestnut lumber is used for structural purposes, caskets, interior trim, furniture, picture frames, and crates. The rough wood is used for fence posts, poles, ties, fence rails and fuel. Although the supply is limited chestnut is still an important source of a tannin extracted from wood chips and used for tanning heavy leathers.

Identifying characteristics: Leaves alternate, six to eight inches long, two to three inches wide, drooping, coarsely toothed, both ends tapered; veins parallel, terminating in each tooth; bark with flattened, continuous ridges; twigs spotted; flowers conspicuous, on pencil-like stalks; fruit a spiny bur enclosing one to three edible nuts.

55

WHITE OAK

Quercus alba L.

T HE NINE SPECIES OF OAK NATIVE TO THE state are important contributors to the wealth and beauty of Michigan's forest land. Most familiar and most widespread of these is the white oak. Though found only rarely in the Upper Peninsula, it is abundant on the slopes and gravelly hills in the north central part of the Lower Peninsula, where it seeded in and sprouted following forest fires, and throughout the south half of the Lower Peninsula.

Although it grows on all but the wettest soils, white oak prefers the dry, hilly, upland type of country. In the southern part of the state it is associated with the hickories, white ash, walnut, red cedar, sassafras, and other oaks. It is often the most abundant tree in the stand. Farther north in the old burned-over pine areas, its common associates are aspen, red maple, white, red and jack pines. Here it frequently occurs in nearly pure stands as well. Best growth is attained in the southern part of the state and farther south, where heights of 75 to 100 feet and diameters of two to four feet are common. White oaks have been found which were 150 feet tall and eight feet in diameter. Such trees may be 800 years old.

A tree which thrives best in the open, white oak produces a broad, round-topped crown, frequently broader than high, with a short trunk and heavy spreading branches. Trees grown under crowded forest conditions, however, produce narrow crowns and long clear trunks especially desirable for high quality lumber. Growth of white oaks usually is slow, although diameter growth of nearly an inch per year is not uncommon in young trees on favorable soils. Desirable as lawn and shade trees, they are difficult to transplant when very large, due to the deep, strong taproot they produce.

On young twigs the bark at first is bright green and hairy, later becoming reddish. On the older branches and trunk it is ash-gray or whitish, broken into small, flat, rather flaky plates, and on old trees may be two or more inches thick.

The leaves occur in clusters of three to five at the ends of the twigs, with others appearing alternately along the twigs. Usually five to nine inches long and about half as wide, they are oblong or spatula-shaped in outline, tapering gradually down the leaf stem or petiole. Varying considerably even on the same tree, some of the leaves may have narrow lobes and be cut nearly to the center, while others may have broad lobes and be very shallowly cut. The ends of the lobes always are rounded, a characteristic of the "white oak group." Occasionally the lateral lobes have an extra finger. Flesh colored when they first appear in the spring, the leaves become bright green and shiny on the upper surface and somewhat paler beneath. They are thin and firm. In the autumn they turn light brown, russet, or purplish red, and frequently remain on the tree throughout the winter. Winter buds are ⅛-inch long, oval, with dark reddish-brown, shiny scales, and are clustered fist-like at the ends of the twigs.

The flowers appear in May with the leaves. Acorn-producing pistillate flowers are small and inconspicuous, while the pollen-bearing staminate flowers hang in tassel-like catkins on the same tree. In the autumn of the first season the short-stalked acorns mature. The brown hairy cup encloses one-fourth to one-third of the nut which is light brown, rounded, about ¾-inch long. The acorns frequently occur in pairs. Sweet and edible, they are an important game food, being relished by squirrels, grouse and other small animals, and in certain localities forming a large part of the fall and winter deer diet. About 150 of these acorns will weigh a pound.

Occasionally in northern Michigan epidemics of an insect known as the walking-stick have caused considerable damage over small areas by defoliating and occasionally killing oaks. Many other leaf eating and gall producing pests, leaf miners, and an insect known as the twig-pruner, cause local concern but seldom are fatal. Several species of fungi cause wood rots in old trees, and a relatively new disease known as "oak wilt" may cause gradual dying in white oaks.

White oak wood is light brown in color, uniformly strong, hard, close-grained, durable and nearly twice as heavy as white pine, weighing 48 pounds per cubic foot when dry. The spring growth of the wood is marked by a narrow zone of large pores characteristic of the oaks. In white oak these pores contain a waxy crystalline substance visible under a hand lens. The wide variety of uses for this wood makes white oak one of the most valuable timber trees of the United States. Most important uses are for furniture, flooring, and interior finish. It is used also for making whiskey barrels, crates, ships, agricultural implements, ties, piling, veneer, pulp and fuelwood.

In volume of timber cut, white oak is not one of Michigan's leading trees. It is, however, one of the most important and valuable species in the southern part of the state. Most of the white oak of commerce is produced in central and southeastern United States, from Ohio to Virginia and Louisiana.

Identifying characteristics: Leaves with rounded lobes, in clusters of three to five at ends of twigs, others alternate, many persisting through winter; bark ash-gray or whitish, flaky; acorns maturing in one year, kernel sweet; spring-wood pores contain waxy substance.

BUR OAK

Quercus macrocarpa Michx.

BUR OAK IS ONE OF THE LARGEST OF THE eastern oaks and has one of the most extensive ranges. A member of the white oak group and similar to white oak in many respects, this species is well adapted to a large variety of soils and is found growing in extremely wet situations as well as on fairly dry sites.

In Michigan the bur oak, or mossy-cup oak, as it is sometimes called, is found principally in the south part of the Lower Peninsula but occurs also in spots throughout the north half of the Lower Peninsula, and in Menominee and Chippewa counties in the Upper Peninsula. Though not so abundant in southern Michigan as white oak, its long straight trunks and high quality timber make it a valuable lumber producer. It is an excellent landscape tree besides, being easy to transplant when young, fairly rapid growing compared with other oaks, and relatively free from serious insect enemies and diseases. It also withstands city smoke and gas better than most oaks.

Bur oak occurs normally in mixed stands or in very small pure clumps. It is never found in Michigan as a predominating species over large areas.

Best growth of bur oak is attained on rich, moist bottomland soils where it may be found growing in association with white oak, basswood, elm, walnut, hickory, sycamore, and soft maples. Under favorable conditions, heights of 70 to 80 feet and diameters of two to three feet are commonly attained. Greatest dimensions are reached in the lower Ohio and Wabash river valleys where bur oaks more than 150 feet tall and seven feet in diameter have been found. When grown in the open, the straight trunk supports a broad irregular crown of stiff, gnarled branches, with the lower ones decidedly drooping. Under forest conditions the crown is rather small and trunk long and clear. The root system is deep, with a strong tap root.

Bark on young bur oak twigs is yellowish brown, at first covered with fine woolly hairs but later becoming ash-gray or brown and smooth after the first season. The twigs and small branches frequently develop corky ridges which disappear on the larger branches. Bark on the trunk is dark gray or brown with prominent, somewhat scaly, parallel, vertical ridges. In winter the tree may be recognized by the extremely coarse appearance of its small branches.

The terminal winter bud is small, usually only 1/8-inch long, conical or ovoid in shape, and reddish-brown. Small lateral buds are clustered near the terminal one.

Bur oak leaves are six to 12 inches long and three to six inches wide, the largest of the oak leaves. The leaf margin is divided into five to nine main lobes, usually rounded but sometimes more or less squared in the case of the two largest. The bottom lobes taper gradually down the leaf stem. The two indentations near the center of the leaf usually extend nearly to the mid-rib. Arranged alternately on the twigs, the leaves are thick and firm, dark green and shiny on the upper surface, pale and somewhat hairy beneath.

The flowers appear in May with the leaves. The male or staminate blossoms occur in yellow-green hanging catkins four to six inches long, usually from the previous year's growth, while the less conspicuous female or pistillate flowers occur on short stalks singly or in pairs at the base of the new leaves. As with other members of the white oak group, the acorns mature in the autumn of the first year. Though variable in size and shape, they generally are round, or nearly round, range from ¾-inch to 1½-inches in diameter, and are covered with soft brown fuzz. The thin cup has a ragged, fringed margin that gives the tree its familiar name. The cup covers at least half and sometimes nearly the whole acorn. The kernel is sweet and edible, making excellent mast. The great range in the size of the seeds is shown by the fact that 35 to 100 of them will weigh one pound.

While bur oak trees are fairly free from insects and diseases of serious consequence, many pests are continually at work on this and other oaks causing local damage to individual trees. The oak webworm feeds on the foliage and clusters of them construct heavy, almost impenetrable bags on the ends of the branches. The gouty oak gall, a rough, hard, scaly and swollen deformity of the limbs and twigs, caused by the larvae of a wasp, occasionally is quite common. The acorns are frequently attacked by various nut weevils. These insects burrow into the developing fruit and lay their eggs at the bottom. The larvae soon hatch and feed on the kernel, gnawing their way out and dropping to the ground when fully grown. In many seasons a large part of the acorn crop is thus destroyed.

Commercially, bur oak wood is sold as "white oak," and the volume and annual cut are a part of the white oak totals. Light brown, with conspicuous rays, it is hard, strong, tough, durable and heavy, weighing 43 pounds per cubic foot, dry weight. Its uses are the same as for white oak: furniture, interior trim, flooring, veneers, vehicles, ties, barrels, crates, piling, caskets and coffins, fence posts and fuelwood.

Identifying characteristics: Leaves 6″ to 12″ long, alternate, with rounded lobes, the two largest sometimes more or less squared, cut nearly to mid-rib in middle; acorns large, fuzzy, maturing in one year; cup fringed, covering at least half, often nearly all of nut, kernel sweet; bark on young twigs often with corky winged projections, bark on trunk with prominent vertical ridges.

57

SWAMP WHITE OAK

Quercus bicolor Willd.

COMMON THROUGHOUT THE SOUTHERN part of Michigan, swamp white oak is found scattered in woodlots and open areas where the soil is rich and where there is an abundance of moisture. It is not of great commercial importance in itself, but serves to augment the supply of "white oak" timber, which in Michigan includes, in addition to this species, bur oak, chinquapin oak, and true white oak. Classified on the basis of leaf characteristics swamp white oak, like chinquapin oak, belongs to the "chestnut oak" group with its toothed, rather than lobed, leaves.

Michigan is on the northern limit of the range of swamp white oak which extends as far south as Arkansas, Tennessee and Virginia. In Michigan it is found as far north as Clare County. While, as its name indicates, it prefers the rich, moist soils of stream banks, swamp borders, and flat, poorly drained pastures, it is found on drier sites as well. Its common associates are red and white oak, white ash, basswood, soft maple, elm, hickory and tulip poplar. Not ordinarily a very large tree compared to other white oaks, it reaches heights of 50 to 70 feet and diameters of two or more feet at maturity. Extreme sizes of 100 feet tall and seven feet in diameter have been reported. It grows fairly rapidly and may attain an age of 300 years or more.

Forest grown trees develop straight clear stems and narrow open crowns with ascending branches. Under such growth conditions straight, clear lumber is produced. In the open this species tends to have a short, buttressed trunk with an open, rounded, somewhat ragged crown and down-sweeping lower branches. Small dead branches often persist low on the trunk.

The bark of swamp white oak is shiny, dark green on the young twigs, spotted with pale lenticels. Later it turns reddish brown and becomes roughened with thin papery scales which curl back at the edges revealing the green inner bark. On the trunks it is thick, gray-brown in color, with deep furrows and long, flat scaly ridges.

The leaves are alternate and clustered at the ends of the twigs. Five to seven inches long and two to four inches wide, they are broadly oval or spatulate in outline, with the widest part just above the middle. The base is tapered and the tip tapered or rounded. The leaf margins are variable. Usually they are coarsely toothed with nine to 15 undulating, rounded, or wedge-shaped teeth. Occasionally, however, some of the teeth may be large enough to be classed as lobes. The bottom one-quarter to one-third of the leaf, where it tapers to the stout stem, is usually untoothed. Thick and firm, the leaves are dark olive green and shiny on the upper surface, and pale to whitish and somewhat downy below. The contrasting colors of the two leaf surfaces give this tree its species name of *bicolor*. The leaves turn dull brown or orange in the fall.

The terminal winter buds are ⅛-inch long, oval or round, light brown and hairy. The laterals are smaller and clustered close to the terminal.

In May, after the leaves have opened, the yellow-green flowers appear, both sexes on the same tree. The staminate or pollen-bearing flowers are in drooping, hairy catkins, three to four inches long, and the pistillate or acorn producing flowers in small, short-stalked clusters. In the fall of the same year the acorns mature. Usually paired or occasionally in threes, they appear at the ends of slender, fuzzy stalks which are one to four inches long, a distinctive feature among our native oaks. The chestnut brown acorns are approximately one inch long, broadly oval and slightly fuzzy at the tip. The bowl-shaped cup encloses about one-third to one-half of the nut, and often has loose scales, especially around the rim. The kernel is whitish, sweet and edible, and is a favorite food of squirrels and other rodents, as well as livestock and deer. A pound of acorns will number 100 to 150.

Swamp white oak has no diseases or insects which are peculiar to it alone, but it shares many pests with the other oaks. It is susceptible to the oak wilt disease which, although it progresses slowly in white oaks, will destroy it, killing a few branches at a time over a period of years. Oak anthracnose is common on this species, curling and blackening the leaves but not killing the tree. Walkingsticks and many other leaf feeding and gall making pests cause concern but are rarely fatal.

As a landscape tree this species is fairly attractive with its low branches and interesting leaves. It is easily transplanted and long lived, but its preference for moist soils limits its use in this field.

The wood of swamp white oak is hard, strong, shock resistant, tough, and heavy, weighing approximately 50 pounds per cubic foot when air-dry. It is close grained with conspicuous annual growth rings. The thin sapwood is scarcely distinguishable from the light brown heartwood.

Commercially, swamp white oak is not separated from the other "white oaks" and its uses are the same, including such items as flooring, furniture, interior trim, paneling, whisky barrels, crates, and farm machinery. Its resistance to decay makes it especially valuable in moist exposed locations where it is used for posts, piling, ties and mine timbers.

Identifying characteristics: Leaves alternate, dark green above, whitish beneath, with nine to 15 rounded or wedge-shaped teeth; bark on branchlets papery, curled back often exposing green inner bark, on trunks deeply furrowed, with flat scaly ridges; acorns maturing in one year, long-stalked, enclosed 1/3 to ½ by bowl-shaped cup with loose scales at rim, kernel sweet.

CHINQUAPIN OAK

Quercus muehlenbergii Engelm.

ONE OF THE LEAST COMMON OF OUR native Michigan oaks is the chinquapin or yellow oak found locally throughout the south half of the Lower Peninsula as scattered individuals in stands of white, bur and red oaks, elm, maple, basswood and ash. Many people know it as "chestnut" oak, a name applied to this and certain other species comprising a small group of oaks which have leaves resembling, in varying degrees, those of chestnut.

Lower Michigan is on the northern edge of the range of chinquapin oak which is found principally from New England westward to the Great Plains and south to Oklahoma, Texas and the Gulf. Though nowhere very common it is most abundant and of some commercial importance in Tennessee, Kentucky, Missouri, Mississippi, Arkansas and Albama. Rocky river banks and rich bottom lands are its favorite locations, but it is often found on dry sites as well. It makes its best growth on soils of limestone origin.

A member of the white oak group, this species has the general appearance and color of the common white oak but does not ordinarily grow as large. At maturity it is a tree of 60 to 80 feet in height and two to three feet in diameter. Maximum heights of 160 feet and diameters of four feet were once reported in the virgin forests of the lower Ohio and Wabash river valleys. Under forest conditions it develops a straight, columnar trunk with a narrow, dense, rounded crown composed of fairly small branches. Trees growing in the open tend to have short trunks and broad crowns. The base of the trunk is frequently buttressed.

On the young twigs the bark is at first smooth and greenish, becoming reddish brown or gray-brown. On older branches and on the trunk it is broken into small, thin, flaky or scaly plates much like that of white oak. Like white oak also, it is silvery or ash-gray in color with a tinge of buff in it. It is generally very thin, seldom exceeding ½-inch in thickness.

The winter buds are cone-shaped, the terminal about ⅛-inch long. The bud scales are chestnut brown in color with whitish, papery margins.

The chestnut-like leaves are variable in size and shape, and are usually clustered at the ends of the twigs. They are four to seven inches long and one to four inches wide, oval in general outline, widest at or just above the middle, with a narrow, pointed tip and a rounded or tapered base. The margins are coarsely but symmetrically toothed with blunt or pointed teeth, each tipped by a minute gland. The leaf veins are straight and conspicuous, terminating in the points of the teeth. Thick and firm, the leaves are lustrous, yellow-green on the upper surface, pale gray-green and finely hairy below. In the autumn they turn orange and scarlet.

The flowers appear in May with the developing leaves. The staminate or pollen-bearing flowers are in drooping, hairy catkins, three to four inches long on the previous season's growth; and the pistillate or acorn-producing flowers in short yellow clusters at the bases of the new leaves. The acorns mature in the autumn of the same year, occurring singly or in pairs, on short stalks or without stalks. They are ½- to 1-inch long, enclosed one-quarter to one-half in small-scaled, bowl-shaped cups. Generally chestnut-brown in color, they may also be dark brown or nearly black. They are usually sweet, the most edible of all acorns. The variation in size will cause the number of acorns per pound to range from 50 to 100 or more.

Chinquapin oak is subject to the same insects and diseases which attack other oaks and particularly members of the white oak group. Fire is one of its worst enemies due to its very thin bark. Among its common insect pests are various leaf miners, the oak twig pruner, walkingsticks, gall insects and nut weevils. It is susceptible to oak wilt disease, and is also attacked by a blight known as oak anthracnose, common on members of the white oak group during damp, cool summers. This fungus causes the edges of the leaves to wrinkle and turn brown or black, and may cause them to drop in mid-season, but is rarely fatal to the tree.

The wood of chinquapin oak is very similar to that of white oak, and it is used for many of the same purposes. The heartwood is brown in color, and the sapwood is thin and pale. Like the other oaks the wood is porous with a distinct line separating the band of large spring wood pores from the summer wood. These pores contain a waxy, crystalline substance found in all white oaks. The wood is hard, strong, close-grained and heavy, weighing approximately 47 pounds per cubic foot when air-dry. It is very durable in exposed locations, and this together with its straight grain and ease of splitting made it especially sought in pioneer days for split rail fences and posts.

Because of its scattered occurrence and generally small size in Michigan this species is of no commercial value here, and of only secondary importance elsewhere. No effort is made to separate it in volume or cut, and it is sold as "white oak," finding its way into flooring, furniture, interior trim, veneers, crates, ties and piling.

Identifying characteristics: Leaves alternate, similar to chestnut, straight-veined, with coarse, symmetrical, gland-tipped teeth; bark ash-gray or buff, flaky, thin; acorns maturing in one year, short stalked or stalkless, sweet, edible, covered ¼ to ½ by bowl-shaped cup.

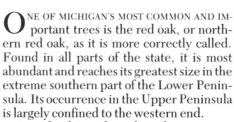

NORTHERN RED OAK

Quercus rubra L.

ONE OF MICHIGAN'S MOST COMMON AND IMportant trees is the red oak, or northern red oak, as it is more correctly called. Found in all parts of the state, it is most abundant and reaches its greatest size in the extreme southern part of the Lower Peninsula. Its occurrence in the Upper Peninsula is largely confined to the western end.

As with white oak, and to a lesser extent black oak and one or two other closely related species, red oak was present in varying amounts in many of the virgin pine forests of the state. Due to its vigorous sprouting ability it has been very important in the rapid natural reforestation of large areas of cut-over and repeatedly burned-over sandy pine land.

Found throughout northeastern United States, northern red oak reaches the northern limits of its range in upper Michigan where, due to shorter growing seasons, sandy soil, and fires, its form and habits of growth vary somewhat from the red oak as found in the southern part of the state. In the north it seldom exceeds 50 to 60 feet in height and two feet in diameter and is relatively short-lived. Farther south straight, clear-stemmed forest-grown trees 70 to 90 feet in height, two to three feet in diameter, and 200 to 300 years old are not uncommon. Open-grown trees have broad, round-topped crowns, and short, thick trunks.

Found on a wide range of well-drained soils, red oak makes its best growth on the rich, moist loam soils of the southern counties where it is associated with elm, basswood, white ash, black and white oaks, beech, walnut, black cherry, and hickory. In the north on the sandy soils its common associates are white oak, red maple, aspen, white, red and jack pines. Red oak makes a desirable street and lawn tree being easy to transplant, moderately fast growing, and fairly free of insects and diseases.

The bark on young twigs and branches is smooth and shiny, at first dark green, becoming reddish and finally dark graybrown on the older branches and young trunks, frequently remaining smooth and unbroken. On the old trunks the bark is broken by shallow grooves into long, usually flat-topped, "ironed-out" ridges. The inner bark is pinkish or flesh-colored. It is not bitter tasting as is the inner bark of black oak.

The terminal winter bud is about ¼-inch long, ovoid, pointed, light brown, and smooth. The lateral buds are slightly smaller.

Botanically, red oak belongs to the "black oak group," distinguished from the white oak group by having pointed instead of rounded leaf lobes, and acorns which mature in two years instead of one. The members of the black oak group are extremely variable in the shape of their leaves and acorns, and are frequently difficult to distinguish. Hybridization is not uncommon among the species of this group. Varying considerably in size and shape even on the same tree, the leaves of red oak are, in general, five to nine inches long and four to five inches wide with seven to 11 broad-based, coarse-toothed, bristle-tipped lobes extending approximately half way to the midrib. Arranged alternately on the twigs, they are thin and firm, dark green and dull or somewhat shiny above, pale green beneath.

The flowers occur in May, when the leaves are about half grown. Both staminate and pistillate flowers are on the same tree, the former in long hairy catkins, the latter solitary and inconspicuous. The acorns, requiring two years to mature, fall during the autumn of the second season, and germinate the following spring. They occur singly or in pairs, are reddish brown when ripe, ¾- to 1-inch long, broadly oval or oblong, enclosed at the base by a shallow, tight scaled, saucer-like cup which seldom covers more than one-quarter of the acorn. White and bitter inside, they are not relished by game as are the acorns of white oak but are eaten to some extent by grouse, squirrels, and deer. Approximately 85 red oak acorns will weigh a pound.

Perhaps the most destructive insect pest of red oak in Michigan is the walking-stick which attacks the leaves of many deciduous trees but prefers oaks, occasionally killing the trees by repeated defoliations. Numerous kinds of gall-making insects feed on the foliage though they are not normally a problem. The most serious disease on this and other species of oaks is the "oak wilt" which kills members of the red oak group in a matter of a few weeks following infection. This unpredictable disease is found in the midwestern states, and was discovered in southern Michigan in 1950, and its range now extends as far north as Grand Traverse and Roscommon counties. It occurs in widely scattered spots, killing individual trees or small groups.

The wood of red oak is reddish brown in color, porous, hard, strong, coarse grained, subject to swelling and checking. The spring-wood pores are large and open. It is used for flooring, furniture, interior finish, barrels, crates, agricultural implements, ties, pallets, fence posts, piling, pulpwood and fuelwood. A cubic foot of dry red oak weighs approximately 45 pounds.

Commercially red oak ranks as one of the most important timber trees of the southern part of the state.

BLACK OAK

Quercus velutina Lamarck

WHILE NOT AS IMPORTANT COMMERcially as some of our other oaks, black oak is a species of common occurrence in many localities in southern Michigan. Another name by which this tree is known is "yellow oak" because of the yellow dye that may be made from the inner bark. Though it occurs principally in the south half of the Lower Peninsula, it is found occasionally as far north as Grand Traverse and Alpena counties.

Black oak grows most commonly on poor, dry, gravelly, upland soils, where it may form a considerable part of the stand. Other trees frequently found growing with it are white and red oaks, hickory, white ash, elm, and red maple. Maximum size of black oak is attained on rich, moist, well-drained soils, but because it is sensitive to competition for light, it is often eventually crowded out of such sites by more shade-enduring species.

Ordinarily it is a tree 50 to 75 feet high and two to three feet in diameter at maturity, but black oaks 150 feet tall and four feet in diameter have been found. When grown in the open the trees are round-topped and limby, with long vertical branches above the slender horizontal or drooping side branches. The taproot is strong and deep. Slower growing and shorter lived and generally of poorer form than many of the other oaks, black oak is little used as a street or lawn tree.

Bark on the young black oak twigs is reddish brown, at first covered with short hairs, later becoming smooth. It is gray and roughened on the older branches and young trunks while old trunks are nearly black, with rough, rounded ridges, deep vertical furrows and cross fissures. The inner bark of twigs and trunk is bright orange-yellow or yellow, and very bitter. It is rich in tannin and at one time was used in the preparation of a yellow dye for coloring wool and silk. Small amounts are used for medicinal purposes.

The terminal bud of black oak is about ¼-inch long, ovoid, light brown and fuzzy. Two or three lateral buds are generally beside it.

The leaves are arranged alternately on the twigs on long petioles. Usually they are five to seven inches long and three to five inches wide. Ordinarily there are seven lobes, though leaves with five or nine are common. Each lobe ends in three or more bristle-tipped or hair-tipped points. The depth of the spaces between lobes varies considerably, but usually it extends more than half way to the mid-rib. This is not a dependable distinguishing characteristic, however, since leaves of black oak are extremely variable even on the same tree. When they unfold in the spring the new leaves are a crimson color. Later they become silvery, and when mature they are shiny dark green on the upper surface and yellow-green beneath. Tufts of rusty brown hairs are found in the angles between the principal veins and the mid-rib on the under side of the leaf.

In May, when the leaves are about half grown, the flowers develop — both sexes on the same tree. The staminate are in hairy catkins four to six inches long, and the pistillate are on short stems, small and inconspicuous.

In the autumn of the second year the acorns mature, solitary or paired. Like the leaves they are extremely variable in size and shape. Ordinarily, they will number 125 to 300 per pound. They are ½- to ¾-inch long, oval, light reddish brown in color, and often striped. The kernel is yellow and very bitter. The cup, enclosing one-fourth to one-half of the acorn, has loose scales above the middle, giving the rim a fringed appearance. Good seed years are infrequent.

Black oak is attacked by the same insects that attack red oak. Among these are the red-humped oak worm, gall making pests, and that curious creature, the walkingstick. In areas heavily infested by this insect, eggs falling on the dry leaves beneath the trees sound like the patter of raindrops. While these pests seldom are fatal to the trees, severe repeated attacks may reduce their vigor and make them more susceptible to diseases. In old trees the "charred fungus" which produces a white spongy rot in the heartwood is very common. Trees damaged by this fungus are commercially low in value. Black oak may be quickly killed by the "oak wilt" disease.

The wood of black oak is similar to that of red oak in appearance and weight. It is reddish brown in color, porous, hard, strong and coarse-grained, with conspicuous growth rings and rays. It is subject to swelling and shrinking under varying moisture conditions. Unless creosoted, it is not durable in contact with the soil. A cubic foot of the dry wood weighs 44 pounds.

Commercially black oak is sold as "red oak," and there are no separate volume or production figures for it. Its uses are the same as those of red oak, and include principally flooring, furniture, heavy construction, barrels, crates, agricultural implements, ties, fence posts, piling and fuelwood. Michigan's commercial production of this species is very small, and it probably does not make up more than ten percent of the total "red oak" produced.

Identifying characteristics: Leaves alternate, variable, usually seven-lobed, lobes bristle-tipped, usually extending more than halfway to mid-rib; leaf stem long; tufts of reddish-brown hairs in angles of veins and mid-rib beneath; bark black with rough, rounded ridges; inner bark yellow, bitter; acorns small, enclosed one-quarter to one-half, maturing in two years; kernel yellow, bitter; cup scales loose above middle.

61

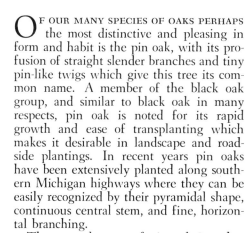

PIN OAK

Quercus palustris Muenchh.

OF OUR MANY SPECIES OF OAKS PERHAPS the most distinctive and pleasing in form and habit is the pin oak, with its profusion of straight slender branches and tiny pin-like twigs which give this tree its common name. A member of the black oak group, and similar to black oak in many respects, pin oak is noted for its rapid growth and ease of transplanting which makes it desirable in landscape and roadside plantings. In recent years pin oaks have been extensively planted along southern Michigan highways where they can be easily recognized by their pyramidal shape, continuous central stem, and fine, horizontal branching.

The natural range of pin oak is rather restricted, extending only as far south as Kentucky and Tennessee west to Arkansas and Oklahoma, and east to the Atlantic seaboard. Southern Michigan marks the northern limit of its occurrence, and although it is found most commonly in the southwestern counties it occurs as far north and east as Saginaw County. It prefers rich, moist bottom lands, but will grow on poorer soils as long as there is plenty of moisture available. It is commonly found in lowlands with other swamp oaks, elm, hackberry, soft maple, and basswood, and, in fact, in many localities is known as "swamp oak." In contrast it is also found growing on light sandy soil with aspen and paper birch in Saginaw County and on old dunes along Lake Michigan in the southwestern part of the state.

Normally a tree 70 to 80 feet in height and two to three feet in diameter at maturity, pin oak may reach sizes up to 120 feet high and five feet in diameter. It makes its best growth in the lower Ohio River Valley. Young trees are distinctively pointed with the branches at right angles to the straight main stem. Larger trees may be pointed or round-topped with the branches spreading like wheel spokes — the uppermost ascending, the middle horizontal and the lower drooping, often to the ground. The lower branches and twigs are tough and persistent, remaining attached long after they have died.

Pin oak bark is dark red on the twigs becoming dark green and finally dark gray, gray-brown or nearly black on the branches and trunk. It is smooth and shiny on the branches and upper part of the trunk, becoming broken only on the lower trunk by thin, tight, scaly ridges and shallow cracks.

The alternately arranged leaves are variable in shape and size and often quite similar to red oak or black oak. In general, however, they are smaller, being only three to six inches long and two to five inches wide, and are more deeply cut, with rounded hollows often extending nearly to the mid-rib. There are five to nine lobes, and as with all the members of the black oak group, the leaf lobes are bristle-tipped. The shiny green leaves become bright red in the autumn, and many are retained on the tree throughout the winter, features which add to its attractiveness as a landscape tree.

In April and May at the time the leaves are developing the flower catkins appear, the male two to four inches long and hairy, and the female shorter, often in clusters of two or three on hairy stalks. The acorns require two years to mature becoming ripe in September and October. Smaller than either black oak or red oak acorns, they are hemispherical, about one-half inch in diameter, slightly broader than high, dark brown in color and often streaked, with a yellow, bitter kernel. The short-stalked cup is shallow and flat, enclosing only the base of the acorn. The cup scales are fine and tight. Approximately 400 acorns will weigh a pound.

The winter buds are clustered at the tips of the twigs with the terminal bud approximately ⅛-inch long, reddish-brown and pointed. The lateral buds are smaller.

A species very similar to pin oak, but lacking its fine qualities, is northern pin oak, also called jack oak or Hill's oak (*Q. ellipsoidalis* E. J. Hill). While its range overlaps that of true pin oak in certain areas, it is generally found farther north in the Lower Peninsula growing on light, sandy, upland soils. The chief distinguishing characteristic is the acorn which is elliptical and covered one-third to one-half by a deep, bowl-shaped cup.

Pin oak has long been a favored tree for landscape plantings in this country as well as in Europe. Its shallow root system and the absence of a prominent taproot make it easy to transplant; and its resistance to city smoke, and even drought, practically assures its survival. Outside of a yellowing of the foliage due to iron chlorosis, and the oak wilt disease, this species has few important enemies.

The wood of pin oak is similar to red or black oak. It is strong, hard, coarse and heavy, weighing 44 pounds per cubic foot when dry. Its color is light brown with thin, darker colored sapwood. Due to the many knots caused by the persistent branches and twigs only the best and clearest trees are cut for lumber for which it is sold as "red oak." Construction material, ties, car blocking, and fuelwood make up most of its uses, with the better quality wood going into flooring.

Identifying characteristics: Leaves alternate, five- to nine-lobed, bristle-tipped, variable, lobes extending nearly to mid-rib; bark smooth except on trunk; acorn small, hemispherical, maturing in two years, enclosed only at base in shallow, flat cup; cup scales tight; young trees distinctly pyramidal with continuous central stem and horizontal branches; old trees similar or round-topped, lower branches drooping; dead branches and twigs persistent.

AMERICAN ELM

Ulmus americana L.

RAPID GROWING AND LONG-LIVED, THE familiar American or white elm, with its characteristic urn or feather duster shape, its gracefully arching branches and drooping branchlets, has always been a favorite landscape tree and has been planted extensively on lawns and streets. One of six species of elm native to the United States and the most important and abundant of the three found in Michigan, the American elm grows naturally throughout the state in areas of hardwood on the uplands, on the more shallow swamp situations and in wet borders along streams. Michigan's two other elms are the slippery elm and the rock or cork elm.

While American elm prefers the deep, rich, moist, loamy soils of river banks and overflow lands, it is found abundantly on soils of less moisture, even on dry sands. Occurring occasionally in small, nearly pure stands which sprang up following fires, elm more often is found in mixture with such trees as ash, hard maple, basswood, aspen, cedar and balsam in the northern part of the state; and with soft maple, hackberry, ash, sycamore, walnut, cottonwood and willow in the southern part of the state. A typical tree of meadows and fields, it makes its best growth under such open conditions.

It commonly attains heights of 75 to 100 feet and diameters of two to four feet at maturity. Heights exceeding 120 feet and diameters over eight feet are found occasionally. Open-grown trees have large trunks which divide rather low into large, upright, arching branches that form a broad, round-topped crown. Forest-grown trees have much longer trunks which do not usually divide until they have reached considerable height, and the crowns are much smaller. The root system of American elm is shallow but spreading.

The bark on the new twigs is at first light green and downy, becoming reddish brown on the older twigs and finally brown-gray to ash-gray on the old branches and trunks. Bark on the trunk and large branches is broken into flat-topped perpendicular ridges, the inner layers of which are alternately light and dark, and somewhat corky in texture.

The lateral buds are ovoid, about ¼-inch long, reddish brown and usually not hairy. There is no true terminal bud.

Arranged alternately on the twigs, the leaves of American elm are oval, four to six inches long and about half as wide, sharp-pointed and double-toothed on the margins. They are thick, firm and conspicuously lopsided at the base. The upper leaf surface is dark green and somewhat rough, while the under surface is lighter green and soft. Prominent parallel veins extend into the main points on the leaf margin. In the autumn the leaves turn yellow before falling.

The flowers appear in March and April before the leaves. Brown to reddish in color, they occur in loose clusters on long stalks. Both stamens and pistil occur in each flower. Seeds mature in May before the leaves are fully developed. Centered in tan-colored, flat, round, notched, hairy-edged wings about ½-inch across, the small seeds are light in weight and are scattered in large numbers on windy days. Drying out easily, few take root except on moist ground. There are 50,000 to 100,000 seeds per pound.

Unfortunately, American elm has many serious enemies. By far the most devastating is Dutch elm disease, accidentally imported from Europe in 1930 on a shipment of elm logs. The disease, which gets its name from Dutch scientists who identified it, is carried by the elm bark beetle. It has gradually spread throughout the East and Midwest; and since its discovery in Michigan in 1950, it has gradually worked its way northward and is now found in every county in the state. Dead elms in cities, rural landscapes and forests attest the severity of this tragic and costly blight, which threatens the very existence of elms. Other pests include cankerworms, leaf beetles and leaf hoppers which riddle the leaves.

The wood of American elm is fairly heavy, coarse-grained, tough and hard. The sapwood is yellowish and thick, the heartwood light brown. It is not durable in contact with the soil, is hard to split, difficult to work, and warps easily. Its hardness and ability to withstand pressure make elm especially useful for agricultural implements and wagon wheels. Other uses include barrel, furniture, veneer, boxes and crates, and truck flooring and racks. A cubic foot of dry elm wood weighs approximately 35 pounds. Michigan and Wisconsin produce nearly half the elm used in the United States.

Identifying characteristics: Leaves alternate, oval, pointed, rough on top, lopsided at base; bark with alternate light and dark layers; trunk divides into upright, arching branches giving typical "urn" shape.

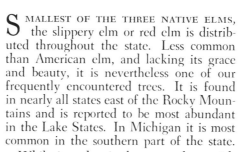

SLIPPERY ELM

Ulmus fulva Michx.

SMALLEST OF THE THREE NATIVE ELMS, the slippery elm or red elm is distributed throughout the state. Less common than American elm, and lacking its grace and beauty, it is nevertheless one of our frequently encountered trees. It is found in nearly all states east of the Rocky Mountains and is reported to be most abundant in the Lake States. In Michigan it is most common in the southern part of the state.

While it makes its best growth on rich moist hillsides, stream banks, and bottom lands, it is frequently found on much drier sites, and particularly soils of limestone origin. Its common associates in our hardwood forests and woodlots are American elm, basswood, maples, white ash, and oaks. It never occurs in pure stands, but always as scattered individuals, usually occupying a dominant position in the stand.

A medium-sized, slender tree, slippery elm seldom exceeds 50 to 70 feet in height at maturity and one to two feet in diameter, although there are records of its reaching 135 feet tall and four feet in diameter under ideal growing conditions. Its thin, rather open crown is not symmetrical like American elm but is usually irregular in outline. The trunk divides, frequently with a U-shaped crotch, into ascending or only slightly arching branches, with the major stems and side branches terminating in more or less separate, flattened or round-topped crowns composed mostly of horizontal or upright branchlets and twigs. It grows faster than American elm, but is seldom planted as an ornamental tree.

The bark is greenish brown and distinctly fuzzy on the young twigs, later becoming gray-brown to dark reddish brown on old trunks, with moderately deep furrows and parallel, flattened, more or less continuous ridges. A knife slice through the thick outer bark reveals its corky, layered structure which is solid brown in color, and not alternately light and dark as in the other two species of elm. The white inner bark next to the wood is thick, fibrous and slippery, forming a mucilaginous mass when chewed. It has a mild odor and flavor suggestive of licorice. At one time it had many practical uses, probably the best known of which was its employment as a thirst quencher due to its ability to stimulate the saliva. Its medicinal properties were also recognized as a soothing agent for raw throats. Peeled off in long strips in the spring and dried, it was later moistened and pounded into a pulp for such uses as wound dressings and poultices for carbuncles and boils. Its tough fibrous structure made it also useful in pioneer days for thongs and lacings. It is still prescribed to a limited extent as a medicine and can be purchased at most any drug store under the name of "slippery elm."

The leaves of slippery elm are distinguished by the sandpaper roughness of the upper surface. Arranged alternately on the twigs, they are broadly oval in outline, five to seven inches long, and approximately one-half as wide, the largest of the elm leaves. They are sharp taper-pointed, widest at the middle, uneven at the base, with short, stout, hairy stems. The margins are sharply double-toothed, and the leaves are often creased along the mid-rib. Thick and coarse, they are dark green and wrinkled above, and paler, occasionally with rusty down, on the under side. They turn dull yellow in autumn.

The winter buds are oval, dark brown in color, approximately ¼-inch long, and covered with rusty hairs which distinguishes them from the smooth buds of the American elm. There is no terminal bud.

In late March or April the flowers appear, developing before the leaves. Clustered on short stalks, they are perfect, containing both stamens and pistils, greenish in color, and inconspicuous. The clusters of seeds mature in May following the opening of the leaves. They are oval to nearly round in outline, ½- to ¾-inch across, with a smooth, papery, veiny wing surrounding a distinct seed cavity. The margin of the wing is hairless, and the tip of the wing is not notched as with the other native elm seeds. There are approximately 40,000 slippery elm seeds per pound.

Of the numerous enemies of this and other species of elm, one is outstanding. Dutch elm disease has caused serious loss of elm trees in the eastern United States, particularly in the urban areas, and has been in Michigan since 1950, gradually spreading into every county in the state. Many insects such as canker-worms and leaf hoppers feed freely on the leaves causing them to be riddled and ragged by mid-summer. Small trees are frequently damaged by the elm scale which is a juice sucker, attaching itself in large numbers to small branches and twigs.

Slippery elm wood is reddish brown in color, with thin lighter colored sapwood, and has a faint licorice odor. It is strong, with a very close grain, and more easily split than the other two elms. The lumber warps easily if not properly piled. It is considerably heavier than American elm and almost as heavy as rock elm, weighing 43 pounds per cubic foot in an air-dry condition. Commercially its wood is marketed with the other elms as "soft elm," and its uses are the same, including farm equipment, truck floors and racks, sills, furniture frames, baskets and crates.

Identifying characteristics: Leaves alternate, oval, broadest at middle, lobes uneven at base, upper surface sandpapery rough; bark with solid brown corky layers; inner bark mucilaginous; trunk divides into ascending, slightly-arched branches; crown flattened or rounded, irregular, open.

ROCK ELM

Ulmus thomasii Sarg.

OF THE THREE SPECIES OF ELM FOUND in Michigan rock elm is the least common. Its range is restricted to the Lower Peninsula, principally the southern half, although it is found as far north as Emmet and Cheboygan counties. Outside Michigan the range extends from New Hampshire to Wisconsin and Nebraska, and as far south as Tennessee. It makes its best development in Michigan and Wisconsin which possess the largest commercial supplies and which in the past supplied British shipbuilders with the best of rock elm timbers for battleships and sailing vessels.

Rock elm, also called cork elm or corkbark elm, grows on a variety of soils and is less exacting in moisture requirements than either American or slippery elm. It is found on well-drained land, dry gravelly slopes, and limestone outcrops, as well as on heavy clay soils and river banks. Nowhere very abundant, it occurs scattered among other hardwoods such as maples, basswood, cherry, beech, ash, and American elm, which are its common associates. It is moderately intolerant of shade and reproduces poorly from seed, although it has a capacity for sending up root sprouts. The roots penetrate deeply into good soils, but are shallow and widespread on light soils.

Not graceful and spreading like the American elm, rock elm usually possesses a central stem which remains undivided well into the narrow, rounded crown. Short, angular, coarse, drooping side branches along the trunk are characteristic of this species and make it readily distinguishable from the other elms. Frequently the lower branches reach to the ground. Forest grown trees are tall and slender attaining heights of 70 to 80 feet and diameters up to two feet at maturity. Maximum sizes attained are 100 feet tall and three feet in diameter. The scraggly appearance of this tree and its relatively slow growth make it not too desirable as a shade or street tree.

The bark on the new twigs is reddish brown and either smooth or hairy. After the first year it develops thick corky ridges which become broken and irregular on older twigs and small branches. While this characteristic is conspicuous on young trees it may be inconspicuous or absent on large old trees. Mature trunks look similar to American elm, but are often rougher and darker. Like American elm the outer bark is made up of alternate light and dark layers.

The winter buds are brown, sharp pointed, and about ¼-inch long, diverging from the twigs. There is no terminal bud.

Rock elm leaves are three to six inches long and approximately half as wide, being broadest just above the middle. The margin is coarsely double-toothed, and the point less tapered than American elm. The lobes at the base of the leaf are nearly even. Thick and firm, they are smooth, dark green, and shiny on the upper surface, pale and slightly hairy beneath. They turn bright yellow in the autumn.

The flowers form in April and May before the leaves, and are perfect, possessing both stamens and pistils. They are few, on long, slender stems arranged in loose, drooping clusters or racemes. The seeds grow as the leaves develop and are dispersed rapidly when mature. They are oval, notched, ½-inch to 1-inch across, the largest of the elm seeds, averaging 7,000 per pound. The broad wing is hairy on the surface and margin, and has a shallow notch at the apex. The seed cavity is indistinct.

While many insects and diseases attack rock elm, none is more serious than the Dutch elm disease which is threatening the existence of all elms. The disease, which is carried by the elm bark beetle, has been in Michigan since 1950, and has caused the loss of valuable street and landscape trees particularly in the southern part of the Lower Peninsula.

Were rock elm more abundant it would be an important commercial tree, but the supply is so limited that it is frequently not distinguished from other elms in lumbering operations. What proportion of the total volume or annual cut of elm is made up of this species is not known. Its greater strength, density, toughness and straight grain make it superior to the other elms for many uses, and certain industries seek it out.

The wood is hard and tough with a high degree of flexibility and resistance to wear and shock. A sound block of rock elm is almost impossible to split with an axe or maul. A cubic foot of air-dry wood weighs 44 pounds, making it the heaviest of the native elms. The sapwood is nearly white, and the heartwood is light brown, tinged with red. It takes a high polish but the grain is not very attractive. Like the other elms the lumber must be dried carefully because of a tendency to warp and twist.

The principal uses are for agricultural implements, wagon wheels, ties, sills, furniture frames, baskets, and crating for heavy articles. It is also used to a limited extent for such items as hockey sticks, javelins, bows and laminated bowls. Years ago it was used in ice boxes, washing machines and kitchen furniture, but today metal has replaced it for these purposes. The toughness of this species was also recognized by the early automobile industry in Michigan where it was used extensively for hubs and spokes.

———

Identifying characteristics: Leaves alternate, oval, broadest above the middle, lobes nearly equal at the base, dark shiny green on upper surface; bark with alternate light and dark layers; corky ridges on twigs; main stem reaches undivided into crown; trunk with short, drooping side branches.

65

HACKBERRY
Celtis occidentalis L.

LOWER MICHIGAN IS ON THE NORTHERN fringe of the natural range of hackberry, a tree that is fairly common in the states to the south and as far west as the Rocky Mountains, but one that is relatively scarce in this state and not very well known. In Michigan hackberry is found scattered in the woodlands of the southern part of the state, and rarely occurs north of the Bay City-Muskegon line. While it will grow on a variety of soils including dry, gravelly slopes, its favorite locations are stream banks and moist, alluvial soils. Here it will be found in mixture with such species as elm, basswood, sycamore, ash, soft maple, and cottonwood.

Hackberry is closely related to elm, and superficially resembles it in leaf and form as well as wood, although the fruit is entirely different. Other names by which this tree is occasionally known are sugarberry, hack tree and nettle tree. Of the nine or more species of the genus *Celtis* in the United States three are shrubs and six are trees, with our native hackberry and the true sugarberry of the deep south the largest and most important representatives.

Under the ideal growing conditions of the lower Ohio and Mississippi River valleys hackberry may reach four feet in diameter and over 100 feet in height. Usual mature sizes, however, are one to two feet in diameter and 40 to 60 feet tall. It may live to be 150 to 200 years old. While forest grown trees tend to be tall and slender, with single straight trunks and small crowns, open-grown trees usually have short trunks and frequently divide into upright, arching branches forming a broad, rounded, elm-like crown.

Hackberry is easily transplanted when young, is long lived, hardy, drought resistant, has a shallow, fibrous root system, and produces good shade. All of these characteristics have made it useful in shelterbelt, erosion and windbreak plantings. It has been used extensively in the southern prairie states where many other trees have failed to withstand the harsh conditions. It is tolerant of city smoke and has been extensively used as a street and park tree in parts of the United States, although not often in Michigan. Its principal drawback as a landscape tree is its susceptibility to "witches' brooms" which are dense clusters of small, short twigs in the crowns of the trees, caused, it is believed, by the combined activities of a small insect and a fungus. Although they do little harm, oftentimes these growths are so numerous and conspicuous as to make the trees unsightly, particularly in the fall and winter when the leaves are gone. Except for witches' brooms hackberry is comparatively free from attacks by insects and fungi.

The bark of hackberry is one of its most unusual and most recognizable features. Greenish at first, the young twigs finally become shiny reddish brown after the first winter. Young trunks are gray and occasionally smooth, but more often they have scattered, corky, warty outgrowths, which develop on older trees into sharp, irregular, hard, broken ridges over the entire trunk giving it an extremely rough appearance and feel.

The light green leaves are arranged alternately on the twigs, and are variable in size and shape but have the same general outline as elm leaves. They are two to four inches long and about one-half as wide, with tapered tips and rounded or heart-shaped, lopsided bases. The margins are coarse-toothed along the sides and smooth around the bases. The leaf stem is short and hairy, and the leaves turn light yellow in the fall. There are three prominent veins in the leaves, and the fine, secondary veins are arranged in a delicate, lacy network making the leaves very similar to those of wild nettle, hence the name "nettle tree."

The green, slender-stemmed, inconspicuous flowers appear on the new spring growth soon after the leaves have unfolded. The staminate flowers are in clusters near the lower part of the shoots, while the pistillate are solitary at the bases of the leaves near the ends of the twigs. Occasionally perfect flowers occur. The fruit matures in September and October and often remains on the trees throughout the winter. It is a drooping, dark purple, cherry-like berry (actually a drupe) about ¼-inch in diameter, with tough, thick skin, and edible, sweet, orange flesh. It has a hard, wrinkled pale brown seed, and is a favorite winter food of many birds. About 2,000 of the cleaned seeds will weigh a pound.

The winter buds of hackberry are ¼-inch long, light brown, and lie flattened against the zig-zagging twigs. There is no terminal bud. A slanting cut through a twig reveals a white, chambered pith.

Hackberry wood is pale yellow in color with thick, greenish-white sapwood, and distinct annual rings, resembling elm in texture and structure. It is coarse grained, limber and shock resistant, and only moderately strong and hard. It weighs 37 pounds per cubic foot when air-dry. It is not durable in contact with the soil. While it seasons well and takes a high polish, it is difficult to work, and its scarcity makes it relatively unimportant as a timber tree. Its uses are much the same as those of elm with which it is usually sold, and include furniture frames, wagons, baskets, boxes and crates.

Identifying characteristics: Leaves alternate, taper pointed, with rounded or heart-shaped bases; margins toothed, except at base; leaf veins prominent; fruit a dark purple berry, persistent through winter; twig pith white, chambered; bark gray; young trunks warty, old trunks very rough with sharp, irregular, hard, vertical ridges; tree form frequently elm-like.

TULIP POPLAR

Liriodendron tulipifera L.

ONE OF NORTH AMERICA'S MOST DIS-tinctive and beautiful trees is the tulip poplar, also known as tulip tree or yellow poplar. Its tall, straight trunk, symmetrical leaves and showy, tulip-like flowers make it easy to recognize, and its crown can usually be spotted well above the general treetop level of the hardwood forests and woodlots where it occurs.

The name "poplar" is in no way correct for this species since it is a member of the magnolia family. Fossil evidence shows that the genus *Liriodendron* was once widely distributed over the northern hemisphere. Today, however, there are only two representatives, one in central China, and our native species.

The natural range of the tulip tree lies east of the Mississippi River in the central hardwood region. In Michigan it occurs in the lower two or three tiers of counties but is found occasionally as far north as Saginaw. Never an abundant tree even well within its range, it occurs scattered in mixed stands of sugar maple, beech, basswood, cherry, oak, and walnut. It prefers moist but well-drained loams but will grow on all but very wet or dry sites.

Under forest conditions tulip trees are characteristically tall, with straight, clear trunks and oblong, open crowns. They attain the greatest height of any of the native broad-leaved trees, frequently reaching 100 feet or more at maturity, with diameters of four to six feet. Maximum sizes of 200 feet tall and 12 feet in diameter have been recorded in the past. Fast growing when young and sensitive to shade, this species rapidly loses its lower branches producing straight clear trunks which yield wide boards free of knots. It has a spreading root system with a deep, fleshy tap-root, and it sprouts readily from the stump following cutting or fire.

The bark of young tulip trees is smooth and greenish gray with conspicuous white lenticels. On old trees it is dark gray, made up of straight, deep furrows and interlacing ridges. It is thin, and easily damaged by surface fires. The inner bark is very bitter and aromatic, especially on the roots, and was at one time the source of a drug used as a tonic and heart stimulant.

Tulip tree twigs are reddish brown in color and, being aromatic, are a favorite browse species for livestock. The pith is divided by hard partitions. The winter buds are ½-inch long, dark red, covered by two large, flattened scales giving it the appearance of a duck bill. Circling the twig just above the round leaf scars are raised scars giving the twig a jointed look.

The leaves are symmetrical, four to six inches in diameter, smooth edged, and mostly four-lobed with a broad notch at the tip. They occur alternately along the twigs on petioles five to six inches long, and tremble in the breeze in much the same manner as the true poplars, hence possibly the name erroneously applied to this tree. They are dark green and shiny on the upper surface, paler beneath, and turn clear yellow in the autumn.

In May and June, after the leaves have appeared, the large, showy, bell- or tulip-shaped flowers bloom. Nearly two inches across, they are composed of six creamy to greenish yellow petals often tinged with orange or red. The fruit is an upright, cone-shaped cluster of winged, four-angled seeds which ripen in September and October, falling away from the central stalk which frequently persists through the winter. Seeds number approximately 15,000 per pound, but germination averages only 15 percent.

Because of its beautiful flowers, interesting foliage and pleasing form the tulip tree is highly prized in landscape work, but it is not often used as a street tree.

Tulip tree is relatively free from serious insects and diseases, although the tulip scale may kill young trees if it becomes numerous enough. Occasionally the leaves may drop prematurely, but this is usually the result of prolonged hot, dry periods and not a disease or insect. A small bark beetle is the indirect cause of a peculiar coloration which appears now and then in tulip lumber. Holes made by the beetle permit stains to enter, producing an array of yellow, green, red, purple, and blue streaks giving the wood the name of "calico poplar."

The lumber of the tulip tree is sold commercially as "yellow poplar" or just "poplar." Years ago it was often marketed as "whitewood," a reference to its white, clear, sapwood. The heartwood is usually light yellow, but often definitely greenish or brownish. It is soft and fairly weak, but stiff, straight grained, even textured and light, a cubic foot of dry wood weighing 28 pounds. It seasons and works well, does not split when nailed, and possesses excellent paint holding ability. It is not durable in contact with the soil, but weathers well in dry situations.

Commercially, yellow poplar is not an important wood in Michigan because of the small quantity available. In states where it is produced in quantity it is converted into a multitude of products including siding, interior and exterior trim, toys, novelties and woodenware, furniture and veneer core stock, boxes, crates, pulpwood and excelsior.

Identifying characteristics: Leaves alternate, symmetrical, four to six inches across, mostly four-lobed with broad notch at top, edges smooth; twigs circled by scars; terminal winter buds duck bill shaped, ½-inch long; flowers tulip-like; young bark gray-green, spotted; old trunks dark gray, deeply furrowed, straight and clean; often taller than surrounding forest trees.

67

BLACK CHERRY

Prunus serotina Ehrh.

BLACK CHERRY IS THE COMMERCIAL timber-producing representative of the rose family. Good specimens of the species are becoming rare in Michigan, for the tree is much sought after today as in the past for its beautiful wood. The other cherry trees native to the state, pin and choke cherry, are small trees valuable mainly as pioneer forest cover and as food for birds and other wildlife.

Though black cherry occurs generally throughout the state, it is found in commercial sizes and quantities principally in the south half and the northwest part of the Lower Peninsula. Never an abundant tree in forest stands, it may be found growing on a wide variety of soils ranging from rich moist loams to dry sands. Its associates in southern Michigan include oaks, walnut, elm, maples, white ash and basswood. Farther north it is found with such hardwoods as beech, elm, maple and ironwood and occasionally with pine, though on light soils it seldom develops to timber size.

Black cherry is a fast-growing tree with a deep, spreading root system. Under forest conditions the crown is long and narrow and the trunk slender, and more often crooked than straight. Being intolerant of shade when mature, this tree usually occupies a rather dominant position in the forest stand where it receives ample sunlight. In the open the crown is broad and rounded and the trunk short. It is one of the hardiest of trees and will grow in extremely cold "frost pockets" where other trees will not survive. It can be grown readily from seed and is easy to transplant, but its light foliage makes it rather unsatisfactory as a shade tree.

Bark on young twigs is smooth, green at first but turning red or reddish brown, with conspicuous whitish, horizontally elongated lenticels, or breathing pores. On older branches and young trunks the bark is dark red or nearly black, frequently peeling off in thin scroll-like strips. On old trunks it is dark brown or black and broken into small thin scales with upturned edges. The inner bark is bright green, bitter to the taste but with a pleasant aroma. Bark of the roots and branches is rich in hydrocyanic acid which is used in cough medicines, for other medicinal purposes, and for flavoring.

The terminal winter buds are ovate in shape, about ¼-inch long, and light brown with visible bud scales. Lateral buds are similar but smaller.

Black cherry leaves are arranged alternately on the twigs. Narrow and oval with a sharp, tapering point, they are three to six inches long and one to two inches wide. The upper surface is dark green and shiny, the under surface pale green and dull. Near the base of the leaf, on the underside along the mid-rib, are tufts of reddish hairs that help distinguish the black cherry from the pin and choke cherry. Margins of the leaves are finely toothed with sharp, incurving

teeth. The leaves usually are troughed or keeled with the edges angling up from the mid-rib. They turn yellow in the fall.

In May and June when the leaves are about half grown the fragrant, pure white, five-petaled, perfect flowers appear clustered along drooping flower stems four to five inches long, on the previous year's growth. The clusters of fruit ripen in late summer and early fall, and bend down the ends of the branches with their weight. The ripe cherries are about the size of peas, dark purple or almost black, with dark red or purple edible flesh enclosing an egg-shaped pit. Four to five thousand of the seeds will weigh a pound. The small five-pointed flower calyx persists on the top of the fruit and distinguishes this species from choke cherry, on which the calyx is absent. Fruits of the pin cherry are on separate stems like domestic cherries. Black cherries are an important food of game birds, especially grouse, and also of song birds, which scatter the seeds widely. Bears and raccoons relish the fruit, and leave evidence of their visits in torn bark and broken branches. Black cherries are sometimes used to flavor rum or brandy.

Black cherry is afflicted with many insect pests, one of the most common being the eastern tent caterpillars which crawl over the trees in droves and frequently devour all the leaves. They build ugly nests in the twig crotches. Among the diseases of black cherry, "black knot" is perhaps most common. Black cherry is easily injured by fires, making it easily susceptible to heart rots, which prevents use of the wood for timber purposes.

Long a favorite among cabinet and furniture makers, black cherry wood still commands a high price on the market. It is hard, easily worked due to its even texture, close grained, strong, warps and checks little in seasoning, and withstands shock and pressure. Reddish-brown in color, it has fine but visible rays and a lustrous surface. A cubic foot of dry cherry weighs about 36 pounds. Its uses include furniture, panels, veneers, handles for saws and other tools. It is the preferred wood of printers for blocks and for backing electrotype plates.

The bulk of the cherry cut in Michigan comes from southern and central area, principally from Tuscola, Shiawassee, Mecosta and Branch counties.

Identifying characteristics: Leaves alternate, narrow, tapered and pointed; reddish hairs along mid-rib on underside near base; leaf margins with fine, incurved teeth; fruit dark red to blackish, clustered on drooping stems, edible, calyx present; bark on young branches aromatic, bitter, dark red, smooth, later peeling, lenticels conspicuous; on old trunks bark broken into thin scales.

KENTUCKY COFFEE-TREE *Gymnocladus dioica* (L.) K. Koch

KENTUCKY COFFEE-TREE IS ONE OF MICHigan's most interesting and most infrequent trees. Never very common, it has gradually been disappearing from the forests and woodlots in the southern part of the state. Because of its scarcity and unusual beauty, it deserves to be protected by public and private landowners, and propagated for planting. It is not so rare in the states to the south, but nowhere is it plentiful.

A member of the legume family, Kentucky coffee-tree is one of only two species of the genus *Gymnocladus*, and the only one found in the United States. The other is a native of China. The resemblance of the round, flat seed to the coffee bean gave rise to the early name, "coffee-tree," by which it was known at the time it was planted in Europe as a curiosity in the mid-1700's. The word "Kentucky" may have been added by early settlers in that area, or during the Civil War, when Kentuckians brewed a coffee substitute from the roasted seeds in the absence of real coffee. Apparently it was a poor substitute. Other qualities, however, were appreciated by the Indians who considered the roasted seeds a delicacy.

Kentucky coffee-tree is a picturesque tree in both summer and winter landscapes. Its graceful, large, twice-compound leaves, and its gray, sharp scaly bark are notable features, while the thick, purse-like pods suspended from coarse, seemingly twigless branches, offer an interesting silhouette against the winter sky. The botanical name *Gymnocladus* is, in fact, a combination of two Greek words meaning "naked branch," a direct reference to the bare appearance of the stout branchlets. This feature is also evident in the names "stump tree" and "dead tree" once applied to it in certain localities.

Depending upon its location—in the crowded forest or in the open—the Kentucky coffee-tree may be a slender tree 60 to 80 feet tall with a long straight trunk dividing near the top to form a narrow, rounded crown; or it may divide near the ground into several branches which form a broad pyramidal crown. Trunk diameters of two to three feet are attained by mature trees. Its natural range extends from New York State and southern Ontario, west to Minnesota and Nebraska, and south as far as Tennessee and Arkansas. Southern Michigan is on the northern fringe of its range, and it is seldom found above Kent or Shiawassee counties. Its natural occurrence has been extended here and elsewhere through plantings. It is relatively free from insects and diseases, a point which favors its more extensive culture.

The bark on the blunt, angular twigs is reddish and shiny, marked with fine lenticels and interrupted by large heart-shaped leaf scars. It becomes light brown on older branches. Twigs reveal a distinctive salmon-colored pith in cross section. The trunks are dark gray and broken into small, elongated, scaly plates with sharp, upturned edges.

The leaves are among the last to appear in the spring and the first to drop in the fall. They are arranged alternately along the twigs, are twice compound, and are one to three feet long, making them the largest of our native tree leaves in overall size. Each of the numerous secondary stalks has nine or more ovate, toothless, short stalked, thin leaflets, two to three inches long. The entire leaf may have well over 100 leaflets. The primary leaf petiole is often red on the upper surface. Its abruptly swollen base is often wider than the twig where it is attached. The open, plume-like leaves cast light shade in which grass can easily be grown. They turn bright yellow at the first hint of fall.

In June after the leaves have unfolded, the whitish flowers develop, male and female on different trees. The male are in short stalked clusters, three to four inches long; the female in long stalked spikes, 10 to 12 inches long. In the fall the distinctive mahogany colored pods mature. They are 3 to 10 inches long, about 2 inches wide, flat, stalked and pointed. The tough leathery cover is often coated with a bluish bloom. The pods contain several dark red-brown, round, flattened, hard seeds, ½ inch to ¾ inch in diameter. These are the "coffee" beans. They are imbedded in a sweet, yellowish green pulp, which becomes soapy when moistened. The pulp has had certain medicinal uses; and the foliage or pods may be poisonous to livestock under certain circumstances. For such gross leaves and pods, the winter buds are unexpectedly small. Scarcely visible, they are tucked just above the leaf base, often imbedded in the bark.

The wood is light reddish brown, medium hard and coarse grained. It weighs 43 pounds per cubic foot. It was used in early cabinet work, and its durability in contact with the soil made it useful for fence posts and railroad ties.

Identifying characteristics: Leaves twice compound, plume-like, secondary stalks and leaflets numerous; overall length may be three feet; leaflets toothless; fruit a mahogany colored, thick, blunt, leathery pod, persistent in winter; seeds large, round, flattened, with smooth, tough, red-brown coat; twigs stubby, with salmon colored pith; bark gray, with sharp-edged plates.

HONEYLOCUST

Gleditsia triacanthos L.

Honeylocust is a comparatively rare, though easily recognized tree. A native of eastern United States, it is the largest of the three species of *Gleditsia* found in North America. In Michigan it occurs naturally only in the extreme southern part of the state although planted specimens are found as far north as the center of the Lower Peninsula.

A graceful tree with arching branches and feathery leaves, honeylocust is easily transplanted and often placed along roadsides and in parks. It is exceptionally free from insects and diseases. Two characteristics, however, keep it from being used more extensively in ornamental plantings: the seeds are contained in long, twisted pods which litter the ground; and the branches and trunk are armed with long, stiff, treacherous thorns. However, both the seedless "Moraine" locust, and a thornless variety are available from commercial tree nurseries.

Gleditsia was named in honor of Johann Gleditsch, an 18th Century German botanist; and the term *triacanthos* means "three-thorned," referring to the branched thorns.

Honeylocust does not like shade, and usually occurs as a dominant tree when it grows in forest stands, or is found standing by itself in the full sunlight of open fields and pastures. It prefers moist, bottom land soils, but also does well on much drier sites, and, in fact, is very resistant to drought. In the prairie states, honeylocust hedges are common both for windbreak and cattle fencing purposes.

When grown under forest conditions, honeylocust is normally a tree 70 to 80 feet tall and two to three feet in diameter at maturity. Individuals up to 140 feet in height and six feet in diameter have been found in other states, but these are rare. Trees growing in the open are short-trunked and have open, round-topped, spreading crowns. Often the trunks divide near the ground into two or more stems. The root system is deep and spreading and root sprouts are common. Unlike most other legumes, the roots of this species add no nitrogen to the soil.

The twigs of honeylocust are stout and zigzagged, with clusters of branched thorns at the joints. The bark on the twigs is greenish to reddish brown and shiny. On the older branches and on the trunk, the bark is iron-gray to black with conspicuous raised lenticels or breathing pores. The bark on old trunks is occasionally smooth but more often broken by deep fissures into long narrow, scaly ridges, or broad flat plates with projecting edges. Clusters of large thorns often occur on the main stem as well as on the smaller branches, making honeylocust no tree for climbing.

The compound leaves are delicate and feathery in appearance, composed of 15 to 30 small oval or oblong leaflets, one to two inches long and half as wide. Frequently the leaves are twice compound; that is, the main leaf steam is branched and the leaflets occur on these branches. The leaflets are very finely toothed, dark green and shiny above, yellowish-green and dull on the under side. The leaf stems are flattened and grooved on the upper surface.

In May or June when the leaves are nearly grown, the inconspicuous greenish-yellow flowers appear. Though small, they are very rich in honey and attractive to bees. The staminate flowers are in many-flowered, short clusters, and the pistillate are in few-flowered slender clusters. Both sexes are found on the same tree.

The fruit is a strap-shaped, spirally-twisted legume, 12 to 18 inches long and about one inch wide, dark reddish brown or purplish in color. The dark brown, hard coated, oval seeds inside are ⅓-inch long, 12 to 14 occurring in a pod. Squirrels and rabbits are very fond of them. About 3,000 of these seeds weigh a pound. The pods contain a yellowish sweet substance between the seeds which gives the tree its common name, and which has been described as tasting like a "mixture of castor oil and honey." When the pods are green, they are relished by cattle and other livestock. Many of the pods are persistent on the trees throughout the winter. Those that fall are often sent rolling by the wind over the bare ground or snow thus dispersing the seeds.

There is no terminal winter bud. The lateral buds are small, usually arranged one above the other, three to five at a place, with the bottom one often barely visible or entirely hidden beneath the bark.

Honeylocust should not be confused with black locust which, though widely planted in Michigan and further spread through natural seeding and sprouting, is not native to the state. The leaflets of black locust are larger, the thorns are small like rose thorns, and the bean-like pods are only three to six inches long and contain four to eight small seeds. Black locust bark is rough, thick and deeply furrowed.

As a commercial tree, honeylocust is of only secondary importance. The wood is reddish brown in color, coarse-grained and hard, and will take a high polish. It is moderately heavy, weighing 42 pounds per cubic foot when dry. Because of its durability in contact with the soil, fence posts and ties are among its principal uses. Other uses include furniture and interior finish work.

Identifying characteristics: Leaves alternate, compound or twice compound with 15 to 30 small leaflets; bark iron-gray with raised lenticels; long, forked thorns on branches and trunk; seeds in long, reddish-brown, twisted pods; winter buds small, three to five in a place.

BLACK LOCUST

Robinia pseudoacacia L.

ALTHOUGH NOT A NATIVE OF MICHIGAN, the black locust or common locust is a familiar tree in the southern part of the state where it has become naturalized as the result of extensive plantings in past years. Its natural range is limited principally to the Appalachian Mountains from Pennsylvania to Georgia, and to the Ozark Mountain region of northern Arkansas where it is associated with white and red oaks, walnut, ash, cherry, and tulip poplar. It is most abundant and attains its largest size in West Virginia. Its adaptability to many soils and climates, its beauty, and its many uses have made black locust one of the most widely planted of American trees. It is now often considered native in many areas far beyond its original range.

Black locust is a member of the pea or legume family and is the only one of three species of *Robinia* in the United States which attains tree size. It was early recognized for its beauty both here and abroad, and has a record of cultivation in this country dating back to 1635. The genus was named in honor of Jean Robin and his son who were gardeners to Henry IV of France, and who first grew it in the Louvre gardens at the beginning of the 17th century, introducing the tree to Europe.

In Michigan black locust is found throughout the south half of the Lower Peninsula. Although often planted farther north, it freezes back where winters are too severe. It adapts itself to almost any soils except those which are excessively dry or poorly drained, and does exceptionally well in areas of limestone origin. Old fields, fencerows and roadsides are its common sites, and dense groves often occur around a parent tree, the result of root sprouting.

Ordinarily black locust grows to 40 or 60 feet in height and one to two feet in diameter at maturity, although individuals 100 feet tall and three feet or more in diameter are occasionally found. It is a fast-growing tree, especially when young, and, like most fast-growing trees, is comparatively short-lived, seldom living over 100 years. The frequently crooked or twisted trunk supports an open, irregular crown. It is intolerant of shade, and where it ocurs in a forest is generally a dominant tree. Its root system is shallow and spreading but may be deep on dry sites.

Black locust bark is thick and very coarse, even on small trees, with long, rounded, interlacing ridges and deep furrows, often spiraling around the trunk. Green and hairy on the small twigs, it later becomes light brown and smooth on young branchlets, and eventually dark reddish to orange-brown or nearly black on the trunk. It contains a poison which can be fatal to livestock.

The feathery leaves are compound, eight to 14 inches long, made up of seven to 19 alternate or nearly opposite short-stalked leaflets. Each leaflet is 1½- to 2-inches long and ½- to ¾-inch wide, oblong or oval in shape, smooth margined, and may be tipped or notched at the end. They are thin, dark green above with a bluish tinge, and paler beneath, turning light yellow in the fall. The twigs are stout, somewhat zigzagging, and armed with short spines or prickles which occur in pairs at the base of the leaf stalks. The small, hairy winter buds occur in clusters of three or four, and are imbedded in the leaf scar, being hardly visible until they begin to swell in the spring. There is no terminal bud.

The showy flowers appear in May or June after the leaves, in drooping clusters four to five inches long. White and fragrant, they resemble pea blossoms and are attractive to bees and other insects. The seeds mature in September and October in flat, light brown seed pods, three to four inches long, which remain hanging on the trees until spring, forming a source of winter food for certain small animals and birds. There are four to eight orange-brown kidney-shaped seeds in a pod. A pound of seeds will number approximately 24,000.

The most serious enemy of black locust is the locust borer which has caused the planting of this tree to be looked on with increasing disfavor in landscaping as well as for wood production. The inch-long larvae of this beetle bore deep into the trunks and branches of young trees, causing them to break or become deformed, and spoiling the wood for commercial purposes. The borer holes open the way for the entrance of several fungi which cause trunk rots and dying tops.

Despite this drawback to the planting of black locust, it is still used extensively in erosion control, in reclaiming wasteland, and for game food and cover plantings. Its spreading roots and sprouts hold the soil on steep hillsides and gullies, where it may form dense thickets ideal for small game. Its nitrogen fixing roots build the soil and permit the eventual planting of other trees or shrubs. Indirectly the locust borer is beneficial to these uses by stimulating sprouting.

Black locust wood is close grained, hard, strong, shock resistant and very heavy, weighing 48 pounds per cubic foot when dry. It is greenish yellow to brown in color with a thin band of pale yellow sapwood. It turns well and takes a high polish, but is difficult to work with hand tools and hard to obtain in long, straight pieces. It ranks with cedar in durability.

Identifying characteristics: Leaves alternate, compound, with seven to 19 small, smooth-margined leaflets; bark dark reddish brown, coarse, deeply furrowed; twigs with short, paired prickles; flowers pea-like, conspicuous, white, in drooping clusters; seeds in short, flat, light brown pods persistent through winter.

SUGAR MAPLE

Acer saccharum Marsh.

Few species are so well known or have such a variety of uses as the sugar maple or hard maple. Since the turn of the century, Michigan has been the leading producer of hard maple lumber in the United States, and this species is today the most important timber-producing tree in the state. Valued not only for its wood, sugar maple is highly esteemed as a shade and ornamental tree; and its sweet sap, referred to in the scientific name *saccharum,* is the principal source of maple syrup, the preparation of which is a small but important industry especially in southern Michigan.

While sugar maple is found commonly throughout the entire state, the largest remaining commercial volumes are located in the hardwood forests in the western end of the Upper Peninsula. Rich moist upland soils are the most favorable for this species although it is easily adapted to poorer, drier sites. Its common associates are beech, yellow birch and hemlock in the northern hardwood forests, and basswood, elm, ash and oak in the southern part of the state. It is very tolerant and small seedlings and saplings will survive years of suppression under dense shade. Slow-growing and long-lived, it may attain ages of over 300 years.

While maximum sizes of 135 feet in height and five feet in diameter are reported, sugar maple in forest stands normally grows 80 or 100 feet tall and two to three feet in diameter at maturity. Forest-grown trees have small crowns and long, slender trunks often 60 feet to the first branch, while open-grown trees have short trunks with many ascending branches forming a broad, dense, oval or pear-shaped crown. The root system is shallow and spreading. As with all maples, the branching is opposite.

The bark on the twigs is smooth, pale brown and marked with small, light colored spots, while on young trunks it is smooth and gray with whitish patches. On old trunks, the bark varies with different trees, ages and site conditions. It may be light gray and broken into long, thick, loose plates or dark gray, shallowly furrowed and tight.

The leaves are arranged opposite one another on the twigs, are three to five inches long and equally as wide or wider, and occur on long, slender stems. Five (occasionally three) main points or lobes, with scattered, secondary points and otherwise smooth margins, help distinguish this species from other maples. The leaves are thin and firm, dark or bright green above, paler beneath, turning various shades of red and yellow in the fall, a major contribution to Michigan's autumn brilliance.

The yellowish-green flowers appear in April and May along with the leaves, both sexes usually on the same tree. The flowers are in crowded clusters on long threadlike stems. The seeds mature in September and October and germinate the following spring. They are paired, with wings about one inch long, spreading or nearly parallel. Good seed years occur at two- to four-year intervals.

The winter buds are small, reddish brown and pointed, the terminal bud not usually over ¼-inch long. The lateral buds are smaller and are opposite one another on the twigs.

Numerous insects attack sugar maple leaves, among the most destructive of which are the forest tent caterpillar, the spring and fall cankerworms, and the saddled prominent. It is also attacked by many kinds of aphids, scales and mites. The sugar maple borer probably does more economic damage than the other insects by attacking the wood and frequently killing trees. Among the diseases, various leaf blights and wilts are common in ornamental trees, while the *Nectria* canker causes considerable damage to commercial timber. Ornamental trees in cities are frequently damaged by smoke and drought, a fact which often limits the use of this species in landscape plantings.

Hard maple is Michigan's leading lumber producer, amounting to about 20 percent of the total saw timber harvested annually. One-third of the hard maple lumber produced in the United States comes from Michigan. The northern hardwood forests in which maple is the principle species comprise nearly five million acres or nearly one-quarter of the state's total forest area.

The wood of hard maple is strong, tough, hard and heavy, weighing 43 pounds per cubic foot when dry. It takes a high polish due to its close, smooth grain. Usually light brown or buff colored, it is occasionally nearly white. Abnormal conditions often produce curly or bird's-eye maple, highly prized in furniture making.

The tough, abrasion- and shock-resisting qualities of hard maple make it useful for such things as flooring for dance halls and bowling alleys, bowling pins, tool handles, spools, bobbins, croquet balls and mallets, and billiard cues. It is also used in furniture and cabinet work, veneer, ties, chemical distillation, charcoal, paper, shoe trees and musical instruments.

Identifying characteristics: Leaves opposite, five lobed, margins entire; bark on twigs smooth, spotted; seeds in pairs, wings one inch long, slightly spreading or nearly parallel, maturing in autumn; winter buds reddish brown and pointed, the terminal buds usually less than ¼-inch long; open-grown trees with dense, oval or pear-shaped crowns.

BLACK MAPLE

Acer nigrum Michx. f.

THERE IS SOME DISAGREEMENT AMONG botanists as to whether black maple is a distinct species, or whether it is merely a variety of our common sugar maple. In recent years the majority has been inclined to regard it as a separate species. While its wood is almost identical with that of sugar maple, its external characteristics will for the most part definitely distinguish it, and many "sugar bush" operators claim that it produces more and better maple syrup.

When viewed from a distance black maple and sugar maple appear very similar in form, both developing round-topped, oval or pear-shaped crowns in open locations, and small, narrow crowns with long slender trunks when growing in the forest. Closer examination, however, reveals a much richer green foliage, a denser crown with heavy drooping leaves, and blacker, tighter bark in the case of black maple.

More limited in its distribution than its close relative, black maple occurs from New England to Minnesota, and south to Missouri and Kentucky. It increases in abundance in the western part of its range. In Michigan it is confined to the southern part of the state, principally the south one-third of the Lower Peninsula. It prefers the low, rich, moist soils of river bottom lands but is found on many other sites. Nowhere abundant, it is, nevertheless, fairly common, growing in mixture with sugar, red and silver maples, bur, white and red oaks, basswood, ash and elm. It is very tolerant of shade, slow-growing and long-lived. Mature trees often attain 80 feet in height with trunks three feet in diameter.

The bark on new twigs is smooth except for numerous conspicuous, warty lenticels. It is at first greenish orange in color, turning gray-brown in the second year. On old trunks it is dark gray or nearly black, with rather shallow furrows, and tight, narrow, rounded ridges. In contrast, the bark of sugar maple is more apt to be light gray, with broad, flat-topped ridges or plates.

Black maple leaves are arranged opposite one another on the twigs, and are the largest of the native maples, being from five to seven inches long and equally as wide or often wider. Generally three-lobed, the leaves may be five-lobed by the addition of two small lobes near the base. The angles between the broad, short pointed lobes are wide and shallow, and the leaf margins are wavy, with the sides usually drooping as if wilted. The base of the leaf is heart-shaped, the lobes frequently overlapping the stem. They are thick and coarse in texture, with the upper surface dull, dark green and roughened with many small veins, while the underside is pale, yellowish green, and covered with soft, velvety down, especially along the principal veins. The leaf stem is usually also downy. When the leaves are mature a pair of leaf-like scales develop at the base of the stem where it fastens onto the twig. In the fall the leaves turn bright, clear yellow.

In May when the leaves are about half-grown the yellow flowers develop; the staminate and pistillate may be in the same clusters, in separate clusters, or on separate trees. They are broadly bell-shaped, approximately ¼-inch long, on slender, hairy stems two to three inches long. In the fall the seeds develop in pairs with wings set wide apart but only slightly spreading. The wings are nearly one inch long, and the smooth, reddish-brown seeds ¼-inch long, similar in size to those of sugar maple.

The winter buds of black maple are about ⅛-inch long, oval, with reddish-brown, somewhat fuzzy scales. When open, the bright yellow inner scales unfold to a length of ½- to 1-inch.

Black maple makes a fine landscape and street tree, having good form, producing dense shade, and holding its leaves well into the fall. Although many insects attack this species, damage is usually not serious. These pests are the same as those which work on sugar maple, and include the spring and fall cankerworms, the forest tent caterpillar, the sugar maple borer, and numerous kinds of aphids, scales and mites. Of the diseases affecting these two species of maples, the most serious are *Nectria* canker, and an attacker of ornamental trees known as *Verticillium* wilt, which causes sudden wilting and dying of the leaves on one or several limbs, or over the entire tree. This wilt is responsible for widespread losses of street and ornamental maples.

Commercially there is no distinction made between black and sugar maples, both being classed as "hard maple" in the lumber trade, and the woods are, for all practical purposes, identical. The heartwood is light reddish brown in color, and is surrounded by a wide band of creamy white sapwood. It is hard, tough and strong, with close grain and uniform texture. It weighs 44 pounds per cubic foot when dry. It turns well, resists wear and takes a high polish.

The tough qualities of hard maple make it the outstanding wood for dance floors, bowling alleys, bowling pins, croquet mallets and balls, shuttles and bobbins. It is also used extensively in toys, novelties, woodenware, shoe lasts, furniture, chopping boards, piano frames, musical instruments, boxes, crates, and numerous other products.

Identifying characteristics: Leaves opposite, large, essentially three-lobed, often broader than long, sides drooping, underside and leaf stem usually fuzzy; pair of small leaflike appendages at base of leaf stem; lenticels on twigs conspicuous; seeds in pairs, wings one-inch long, slightly spreading, maturing in autumn; bark dark gray to black, with rounded, tight, narrow ridges.

73

RED MAPLE

Acer rubrum L.

Autumn in northern Michigan is remembered by many persons principally for its striking mixtures of colors—the dark greens of the conifers, yellows of the aspens, and scarlets of the red maples. Appropriately named, red or scarlet maple, as it is often called, wears something red the year around—red flowers and newly opened leaves in the spring, red twigs and leaf stems in the summer, red leaves in the fall, and red buds in the winter. Though of secondary importance commercially in Michigan, red maple is nevertheless a useful timber tree and is a desirable species for its beauty alone if nothing else. It is widely planted as an ornamental tree for its form and coloring.

Found throughout the eastern United States, red maple has the widest distribution of any of the maples. Greatest commercial quantities are found in the lower Mississippi valley, and greatest sizes are attained in the Ohio River basin. While it occurs throughout Michigan, the principal commercial stands are in the Upper Peninsula. It is one of seven maples native to the state, two of which—the mountain maple and the striped maple—are usually small understory trees. Another, the box elder or three-leaved maple, is of no commercial value.

Red maple produces its best growth in wet to swampy lowlands, often in areas which are inundated part of the year. In northern Michigan, however, it is very often found on much drier soils in mixture with oak, aspen, and pine, but it does not make its best growth on such sites. Under ideal growing conditions, it attains heights of 60 or 70 feet and diameters of one to two feet. Occasionally, though not in Michigan, it reaches 125 feet in height and five feet in diameter. The slender, graceful branches generally have an up-sweep, forming a narrow rounded, or tapered, rather open crown. It is a rapid-growing species but is short-lived, maturing at 70 to 80 years, and is not as tolerant as sugar maple. The root system is shallow and spreading, and both root and stump sprouts are common. The young sprouts are a favorite food of deer.

The bark on the twigs is bright red to dark red, shiny and dotted with small spots. On the branches, the bark is smooth and light gray, becoming dark gray on the trunk, with shallow cracks and narrow ridges separating into plate-like scales. On open-grown shade trees, the bark may be black and tight.

The leaves are two to six inches long and equally as wide, on long, reddish stems. Usually having three lobes, they may have five if the two basal lobes are large enough to count. The space between the lobes is shallow and the angle is wide. The entire leaf margin is coarsely and irregularly toothed. Red when they first begin to appear in the spring, the leaves become bright green above and pale green or whitish below. Autumn turns them to scarlet and varying shades of red, orange, and yellow.

Appearing long before the leaves, the small but conspicuous red flowers are among the first signs of spring. They are long-stemmed and in small clusters, both staminate and pistillate usually, though not always, on the same tree. Of the five tree-size maples in the state, red maple produces the smallest seeds, 18,000 being needed to weigh a pound. They mature in May and June, are paired, with reddish wings approximately ¾-inch long, spreading to form nearly a right-angle at the top. They germinate quickly after falling.

The winter buds are dark red, blunt, the terminal bud about ⅛-inch long, and the lateral buds somewhat smaller, occurring in opposite pairs.

While many insects attack the leaves of red maple and cause concern where ornamental trees are infested, seldom do such attacks prove fatal. Gall producers, such as the maple bladder gall mite, cause peculiar spots and disfigurations on the leaves. The cottony maple scale is very common and often quite injurious to small trees. Both spring and fall canker worms are common leaf feeders. The most injurious of the wood fungi is the white heart decay caused by *Fomes igniarius* which enters and spreads rapidly from bark wounds or branch stubs. A leaf disease called "tar spots" often causes the leaves to drop prematurely but seldom does any serious damage.

From a commercial standpoint, red maple ranks with silver maple in importance. It is classed as a "soft maple" along with silver maple. Red maple attains greater commercial importance in states farther south.

The wood of red maple is hard, brittle, close-grained, with light brown heartwood and wide, white sapwood. It is not as heavy or strong as hard maple, a cubic foot of dry wood weighing 38 pounds; but it is somewhat heavier and stronger than silver maple. Its principal uses include box lumber, ties, woodenware, veneer, furniture, flooring, chemical wood and charcoal.

Identifying characteristics: Leaves opposite, usually three-lobed but occasionally five-lobed, margins irregularly toothed, turning scarlet in autumn; seeds paired, wings ¾-inch long, the two wings forming nearly a right angle, mature in spring; winter buds ⅛-inch long, dark red, blunt; bark on twigs red, spotted; branchlets opposite.

SILVER MAPLE

Acer saccharinum L.

A TYPICAL TREE OF THE RIVER BANKS AND low, moist woods of southern Michigan, silver or soft maple is one of the state's most beautiful and ornamental trees. Because it is fast growing and graceful, it has been widely planted throughout the state as a street and lawn tree. Recently its use in cities has been discouraged because storms break off the brittle branches, and because its profusion of roots frequently clog drains and sewers in search of water.

Found naturally only in the south half of the Lower Peninsula, silver maple occurs only rarely north of Saginaw Bay. It occurs always in mixed stands, and its associates in its natural habitat of rich bottom land soils—often inundated during periods of high water—are such species as elm, swamp white oak, willow, box elder, black walnut, hickory, sycamore, cottonwood and hackberry. Shallow-rooted, it grows best where an abundance of moisture is available, but adapts itself to a variety of soils.

Silver maple reaches heights of 60 to 80 feet or more at maturity, with diameters of two to four feet. Frequently the trunk separates near the base into three or four large, upright, spreading limbs which form a broad, frequently elm-like crown. The gracefully drooping, oppositely arranged branchlets have a decided upward sweep at the ends. Trunks of trees growing in forests are clear of branches to a considerable height, while more open-grown trees may have low-hanging branches that nearly touch the ground.

The bark on young twigs is smooth, reddish gray and shiny, and the twigs have a rather rank odor when broken. On the young branches and trunks of young trees the bark is silver-gray with a brownish tinge and smooth; becoming, on older branches and trunks, dark gray to brown, shallowly grooved, with long, loose, scaly plates which are unattached at the ends, and which frequently flake off.

The terminal winter buds are ¼-inch or less in length, dark red in color and blunt. As with all maples, the leaves of silver maples are arranged oppositely along the branchlets. They are sharp-toothed along the margins and distinctly five-lobed. The depth of the incisions between the lobes varies from one tree to another. Leaves of the "cut-leaved" maple (*A. saccharinum* var. *Wieri*) are cut nearly to the mid-rib. Three to six inches long and nearly as broad, the leaves occur on long, slender, drooping petioles. They are light green on the upper surface and silvery-white beneath, turning upward in the breeze to give the tree the silvery cast from which it gets its name.

Silver maple is one of the first trees to bloom in the spring, the flowers appearing in March or April. The dense clusters of yellow to red staminate and pistillate flowers may occur separately on the same tree, or the two kinds of flowers may be on separate trees, in which case only the trees having pistillate or female flowers produce seeds. The flowers mature and the fruit forms about the time the leaves are fully grown. The seeds soon fall, and germinate shortly after they reach the ground. They are tan colored, paired, with widely divergent, incurved wings, 1½- to 2-inches long, one seed and wing frequently being only partly developed. Largest of the northeastern maple seeds, only 1,200 to 1,500 seeds of this tree are required to make one pound.

Silver maple is very susceptible to decays which enter and spread rapidly from bark wounds or breaks caused during wind or ice storms. The common white heart decay causes considerable damage and frequently renders whole stands worthless as timber. Tar spots on the leaves may cause early defoliation but do no permanent damage. Many species of insects and mites attack the leaves, some like the bladder gall, forming warty growths, others cause discolorations, curling or distortion, and defoliation. While these insect pests cause much concern where ornamental trees are attacked, cases where they prove fatal to the trees seldom occur.

Due to the relatively limited and generally mixed occurrence of this species, silver maple cannot be classed as a type in itself, but is one of the species included in the ash-elm type. Commercially this species is not separated from red maple, both being termed "soft maple."

The wood of silver maple is hard, close-grained, strong, brittle, and easily worked. It is pale brown in color with lighter colored, thick sapwood. Its uses in Michigan include lumber, crate and fish box stock, furniture, veneer, woodenware and fuel wood. A cubic foot of the dry wood weighs 34 pounds. Occasionally the trees are tapped for maple sap, but their use for this purpose does not compare with that of the hard maples which produce twice as much sugar from the same amount of sap.

Identifying characteristics: Leaves opposite, distinctly five-lobed, margins sharply toothed, silvery on under side; seeds 1½- to 2-inches long, double, one side often undeveloped, maturing in spring; branchlets opposite; branches ascending; bark on branches and young trunks silvery-gray.

75

NORWAY MAPLE

Acer platanoides L.

URBAN DWELLERS IN MICHIGAN AND the eastern United States are probably more familiar with the Norway maple than any of the native maples since it is the most commonly planted shade and street tree in this region. Its rapid growth, pleasing form, ability to withstand city smoke and dust, and relative freedom from serious insects and diseases make it one of the best trees for landscape purposes.

Norway maple is an import from central Europe where it is one of the common hardwoods in the forests of that region. It was introduced into England in 1683 and records of planting in America date back to colonial times. It is found today along streets and roadsides and in parks and yards throughout the eastern part of the country, in the Rocky Mountain area, and along the west coast. It is becoming naturalized through self-seeding in some parts of the East. Many varieties are recognized, the most familiar of which is the Schwedler maple (*Acer platanoides* var. *schwedleri*) whose leaves are bright red when they open in the spring, gradually turning to bronze and finally to a deep purple-green with red veins and stem.

While preferring rich, well drained soils, Norway maple will grow satisfactorily on a variety of sites. It is propagated easily from seeds, grows rapidly, especially when young, developing a low-branching, rounded crown of stiff branches and coarse, straight, opposite twigs. Heights of 60 feet and trunk diameters of two feet are attained at maturity. Its very dense foliage and network of fine surface roots, may cause lawn problems, resulting from shade, interception of rain, and competition for soil moisture. Pruning the lower branches at an early age, however, not only produces a clear straight trunk, but also develops the crown well above the ground thus permitting both moisture and light to reach the soil beneath.

The bark on the new twigs is smooth and shiny, green to reddish-brown in color and dotted with light colored lenticels. On the young branches it is light gray-brown, and on the trunks it is dark brown, with closely spaced, shallow, vertical grooves, and smooth, tight, narrow ridges.

Norway maple leaves are larger than those of any of the native maples, being from five to eight inches long and equally as wide or somewhat wider. They are arranged opposite one another on the twigs. The leaf stems are three to six inches long, and when broken exude a white milky juice which is positive identification of this species. Normally the leaves have five major lobes with many secondary points, although they may occasionally have seven lobes. They are among the first leaves to come out in the spring, and they remain one to two weeks longer than most other leaves in the fall, frequently dropping after the first snows. Although they may remain green throughout this season, they usually turn to pure yellow, and often, following a still, frosty night, drop heavily forming a thick blanket directly beneath the tree.

Before the leaves develop in May or June, the yellow-green flowers appear in rounded clusters at the ends of the twigs. The largest and most conspicuous of the maple flowers, they are approximately ¼-inch across. They have five sepals and five petals; some are perfect, some contain only stamens, and some only pistils. The seeds are full grown by early summer, ripening in the fall. They are in winged pairs, 1½-inches long, on long drooping stems, the upper edge of the two wings forming nearly a straight line. They are formed abundantly and take root easily. About 2,600 seeds will weigh a pound.

The terminal winter buds are dome-shaped, about ¼-inch long, with yellow-green to red, paired, shiny scales which have keel-like ridges. The lateral buds are small, and lie flat against the twigs. When cut, the buds produce a milky juice.

While Norway maple is considered to be more resistant to insects and diseases than the native maples, it, nevertheless, is attacked by many pests. Probably the most serious enemy is the *Verticillium* wilt disease which causes the leaves to suddenly wilt on part or all of the tree, and may cause it to die. Branch tips in the tree tops are sometimes killed by a canker disease which is apparently related to winter injury. Larvae of the tussock moth may partially defoliate trees, and a leaf stem miner or petiole borer may cause concern by causing leaves to drop in mid-summer. Aphids and plant lice often become abundant causing droplets of "honey-dew" to deposit on sidewalks or automobiles beneath, but doing little harm to the trees.

The wood of Norway maple is softer than that of sugar maple but harder than silver maple. It is reddish white to buff colored, even textured, straight grained, and takes a high polish. It has no commercial value in this country, but in Europe it is cut into lumber and veneer, and is used for such articles as furniture, wooden kitchenware, brush backs and turnings. A cubic foot of dry Norway maple wood weighs approximately 41 pounds.

Identifying characteristics: Leaves opposite, with five major lobes, margins with many secondary points; leaf stem long, exudes milky juice when broken; lenticels on twigs conspicuous; seeds in pairs, upper margin of wings forming nearly straight line, maturing in autumn; bark finely furrowed.

BOX ELDER

Acer negundo L.

Although seldom seen in its native habitat in Michigan, box elder is nevertheless one of our most commonly observed trees. It is found naturally only along river courses in the south part of the state, but has been planted so extensively along city streets, on farms and countrysides that it is rarely thought of as a wild species.

This poor relation of the maples, which has little in common with them except the seeds and sap, is not an attractive tree by most standards, and its wood has little commercial value. Yet it has served man well. Its adaptability to nearly all sites, its ease of transplanting, fast growth and drought resistance, made it a valuable landscape and street tree for rapidly expanding cities, and a source of shade and protection to prairie settlers. Spreading box elders still dominate the yards of many an old Michigan farmstead. It is still planted today for shelterbelts and for game food and cover, but its use as a landscape or street tree has greatly decreased in favor of more attractive, longer-lived species. Several varieties of box elder, however, are still used for ornamental purposes, particularly in the Northwest.

The natural range of box elder, or ash-leaved maple as it is sometimes called, extends south to Florida and central Texas, and west to the eastern slopes of the Rocky Mountains. Nowhere abundant in Michigan, it is found naturally only as far north as Saginaw Bay, and is most frequent in the southwestern part of the state. The deep, wet soils of riverbanks and swamp borders are its natural sites, and in such localities it is associated with cottonwood, willows, hackberry, sycamore and silver maple.

Ordinarily a tree 30 to 50 feet in height with a crooked trunk one to two feet in diameter at maturity, box elder may attain a height of 70 feet or more with a short massive trunk four feet through. It frequently divides near the ground into diverging stems forming a broad, unsymmetrical crown, composed of straight or upward-arching, limber branches and coarse, oppositely arranged twigs. It has a shallow, spreading root system, and it sprouts vigorously from stumps or surface roots, the stout canes often growing four to five feet tall in one year. A mild maple sugar can be made from box elder sap, but it lacks the sweetness and flavor of that made from sugar maple.

The bark on box elder twigs and sprouts is smooth, green to brown or purple in color, shiny or covered with a waxy bloom, and spotted with small lenticels. It is greenish brown or buff colored and slightly roughened on the young branches and small trunks; and on old trunks gray-brown to dark brown, with narrow rounded or flattened, interlacing ridges separated by narrow to broad, shallow fissures.

Arranged opposite one another on the twigs, the leaves of box elder are pinnately compound, usually with three to five leaflets, but occasionally with seven or nine. The leaflets are two to four inches long and 1- to 2½-inches wide. Variable in shape, they range from oval to lance-shaped, with long tapered points, and margins which may be nearly smooth, coarsely toothed, or three-lobed. They are dull, light green on the upper surface and paler beneath, turning dull yellow in the fall and dropping early. The leaf stems are slender with enlarged bases which leave raised, crescent-shaped scars completely surrounding the twigs.

The terminal winter bud is ⅛- to ¼-inch long, enclosed in two dull red scales. The lateral buds are smaller and in-curved. The small, yellowish-green flowers appear in April or May before or with the developing leaves, on heavy, threadlike stems, the two sexes on separate trees. In early summer the paired seeds develop in dense drooping clusters which may remain on the trees until the following spring. The seeds are narrow and pointed, and the V-shaped pairs of wings, 1- to 1½-inches long, curve in toward each other at the ends. The availability of the seeds during the winter makes them a valuable food for many birds and squirrels. There are an average of 12,000 seeds per pound.

While box elder is subject to the attacks of many of the same insects and diseases which attack maples, the pest which causes the most attention is the box elder bug. This creature is known more as a household pest than because of the injury it does to the trees. The adults are harmless bugs about ½-inch long, and dark gray bordered with red. In the fall they swarm in great numbers on the trunks of the female flower producing trees, later crawling on walls, into cracks, or entering houses in search of winter hibernating places. The eggs are laid in the spring, and the bright red, immature bugs feed during the summer on box elder leaves, but seldom cause noticeable damage to the trees.

The wood of box elder is soft, weak and close-grained with creamy-white heartwood and a wide band of scarcely distinguishable sapwood. It is very light in weight, weighing only 27 pounds per cubic foot in an air-dry condition. Of little or no commercial value today, it is used to a limited extent in the manufacture of woodenware and furniture frames. It is also used for paper pulp and, of course, for fuelwood.

Identifying characteristics: Leaves opposite, compound, with usually three to five oval or lance-shaped leaflets; margins may be smooth, coarse-toothed, or lobed; twigs greenish to purple, smooth, often with waxy bloom; seeds in clusters, paired, 1- to 1½-inches long, wings curving in, persistent through winter; crown irregular, trunk crooked.

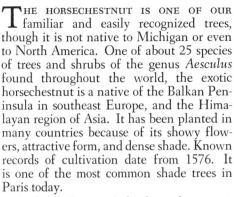

HORSECHESTNUT

Aesculus hippocastanum L.

THE HORSECHESTNUT IS ONE OF OUR familiar and easily recognized trees, though it is not native to Michigan or even to North America. One of about 25 species of trees and shrubs of the genus *Aesculus* found throughout the world, the exotic horsechestnut is a native of the Balkan Peninsula in southeast Europe, and the Himalayan region of Asia. It has been planted in many countries because of its showy flowers, attractive form, and dense shade. Known records of cultivation date from 1576. It is one of the most common shade trees in Paris today.

A close relative of the horsechestnut is the Ohio buckeye from which that state gets its nickname. The buckeye is occasionally found in the extreme southwestern part of Michigan. The large rounded seeds of both the buckeye and the horsechestnut have a whitish spot making them resemble the eye of a buck deer. The derivation of the name "horsechestnut" is not so apparent. The botanical name of the species comes from two Latin words: *hippo* meaning horse, and *castanum* meaning chestnut. However, the species is not a chestnut, and the bitter seeds are not particularly palatable to horses. Perhaps the name stems from the onetime use of the seeds as a horse medicine; or from the horse-hoof shape of the large leaf scars.

Horsechestnut has been planted throughout the United States, and it can be found in all parts of Michigan, although it is most common in the southern part of the state. It is not as popular today as in former years when it was commonly planted as a park or landscape tree. Horsechestnut needs space, and is not too desirable on lawns or along streets where its heavy litter of nuts may be a nuisance. While mature trees growing on ideal sites may attain heights of 80 to 100 feet, with diameters of three feet, trees more commonly seen in Michigan are 40 to 60 feet tall and one to two feet in diameter. The trees grow rapidly on a variety of soils, forming a broad dome-shaped crown with gracefully upsweeping branches, and coarse, zig-zagging branchlets. It is easy to propagate and transplant, and several horticultural forms are recognized as a result of both natural and artificial hybridization.

The bark on the twigs is reddish brown, smooth, and dotted with large whitish lenticels. On the older branches and trunks it becomes dark gray-brown and broken into thin, irregular, small plates or scales. Very bitter tasting, it is rich in tannin and sugar yielding compounds. Decoctions of the bark were at one time used in preparing a yellow dye, and in medicines and tonics.

The winter buds of horsechestnut are among the largest and most distinctive tree buds. The terminal bud, which produces both flower cluster and leaves, is ½- to 1-inch long, rich purple-brown to black in color, and covered with a shiny, resinous gum. The leaf buds are smaller and set opposite one another along the twigs, each above a conspicuous, hoof-shaped leaf scar which contains seven small dots in a semicircle.

The oppositely arranged leaves are compound, composed of seven leaflets radiating spoke-like from the end of a long, grooved, swollen-based stem. (The buckeye has only five leaflets.) The leaflets are four to eight inches long, tapered toward the base, and blunt pointed, with irregularly toothed margins. They are dark green on the upper surface, and paler beneath, turning rusty yellow in the fall. The bottom pair is usually smaller than the others.

In June or July after the leaves are full grown, the showy flowers appear. They occur like candelabras in six to 12 inch upright pointed clusters at the ends of the twigs. Each flower is about ¾ inch long, composed of five white petals spotted with yellow and purple. Some of the flowers are perfect, while some contain only pistils and some only long, yellow stamens.

When fully developed in September, the fruit of horsechestnut is a heavy, round, spine-covered green ball about two inches in diameter. The thick coat splits into three sections revealing one to three large reddish-brown seeds with coats which shine like polished leather. The pale yellow kernel inside is very bitter. At one time the seeds were powdered and used as a soap. They were also once collected on a commercial basis in France for the production of starch. A book-binders' paste made of it was said to keep "book-worms" away.

Very few insects and diseases bother horsechestnut. The white-marked tussock moth may cause minor defoliation, and oystershell scale may kill small twigs, but neither of these will normally harm the trees. Diseases known as "leaf scorch" and "leaf blotch" cause discoloration of the leaves, and where serious may cause them to drop prematurely.

The wood of horsechestnut is creamy-white to yellow, with fine, uniform texture, often cross-grained or wavy-grained. It is soft and weak and not durable; but its light color and ease of working have made it useful in European countries for brush backs, dairy and kitchen utensils, food containers, turned articles, small carvings and artificial limbs. The seasoned wood weighs about 32 pounds per cubic foot.

Identifying characteristics: Leaves opposite, compound, composed of 7 whorled leaflets, tapered toward the base and abruptly pointed, margins bluntly toothed, stems grooved; flowers white, in showy upright clusters; seeds large, red-brown, shiny, in a round, thick, green, spiny cover which splits into three sections; bark dark brown, broken into thin plates.

BASSWOOD

Tilia americana L.

Of the more than fifteen species of the genus *Tilia* found in the United States, only two attain commercial size and abundance, and one of these is the familiar basswood or linden native to Michigan. The name basswood probably is a corruption of "bastwood," referring to the fibrous inner bark or bast which was, and to a small extent still is, used in making cords, mats, and similar articles. Easy to transplant, rapid growing and symmetrical, basswood makes a highly desirable landscape tree. The fragrant flowers are especially attractive to bees, and basswood honey is well known for its unique flavor. Smaller, exotic species such as European and Japanese basswoods are finding much favor in this country as ornamentals.

Found in hardwood regions throughout the state, the native basswood grows commonly on the more moist soils in mixture with such trees as elm, beech, hard maple, yellow birch, black cherry, and, in the extreme southern part of the state, soft maple and some of the oaks as well. Best growth is attained on rich loamy soils with moderately slow drainage, such as may be found on lake and stream borders. Basswood stumps are extremely vigorous sprouters, and deer and rabbits browse on the tender young shoots produced in abundance following logging operations. Clumps of three or four large basswoods are a common sight, showing that these trees originated from sprouts rather than seeds. Small suckers are common even at the bases of living, healthy trees.

Fairly tolerant of shade when young, basswoods develop rapidly under favorable growing conditions, forming at maturity trees 70 to 80 feet or more in height and two or three feet in diameter with straight, columnar trunks and oval or rounded, dense crowns. The branches are slender and straight, with small twigs somewhat zig-zagged. The root system is deep and spreading.

Bark on young twigs is bright red to greenish in color, smooth and shiny, becoming grayish but remaining unbroken on older branches and young trunks. On old trunks it is dark gray, broken by shallow, nearly parallel fissures into narrow, flat-topped ridges roughened by horizontal cracks. Indians used the bark of young shoots for rope making.

Broadly heart-shaped with unequal sides, the leaves of basswood are five to six inches long and nearly as broad, coarse-toothed, dull and dark green above, paler and somewhat shiny beneath, and arranged alternately on the twigs. Tufts of rusty hairs usually appear in the angles of the principal veins on the under side of the leaf.

In the autumn the leaves turn a mottled brownish yellow. The winter buds are about ¼-inch long, rounded and red. When the leaves are absent these red buds will quickly identify this species.

In June and July after the leaves have formed, the creamy-white, downy, fragrant flowers appear in loose, drooping, few-flowered clusters on stalks suspended from the center of narrow, leaf-like bracts which are four to five inches long. The flowers are about ½-inch long, five-petaled and perfect—that is, both stamens and pistils occur in each blossom. The fruits, mature in Sepember and October, are about the size of a pea, round and woody, greenish gray to brown in color, and woolly. They often remain on the trees far into the winter, furnishing food for grouse, quail, squirrels and other rodents. There are about 6,000 seeds in a pound.

Basswood is a favored host of many pests. Among the defoliators the spring and fall cankerworms and the white-marked tussock moths are perhaps the most common. They seldom are fatal to the trees, however. The linden borer frequently does permanent injury by tunneling into the trunk near the ground. Entrance of canker disease often is made possible by woodpeckers riddling the soft bark in search of insects. The hollows caused by fires and rots are commonly used by squirrels, raccoons, opossums and rabbits for dens, and old hollow trees should be favored in farm woodlots for this reason.

The wood of basswood is light in weight (about 25 pounds per cubic foot, dry weight), soft, close-grained, weak, flexible, light reddish brown to white in color. It is not durable in contact with the soil. The ease with which it can be worked, its light weight, light color and lack of odor make it well suited for such uses as venetian blinds, toys, woodenware, yardsticks, drawing boards, frames for comb honey, berry baskets, boxes and crates for cheese, and other food products. It is used also for fuel and lumber, and is the most important source of excelsior. The greatest commercial volumes of basswood are found in the farm woodlots in the south half of the Lower Peninsula.

Identifying characteristics: Leaves alternate, broadly heart-shaped, unequally lobed, sharply toothed; winter buds red; bark grooves shallow, parallel, ridges narrow, flat, transversely cracked; flowers and fruits suspended from narrow lefy bract; old trees commonly suckered at base.

WHITE ASH

Fraxinus americana L.

WHITE ASH IS ONE OF THE MOST valuable timber trees in the United States, and is the largest, most important and most abundant of the six ash species which attain commercial size. The character of the wood makes it ideal for many articles for which other woods are less suited, such as athletic equipment, long tool handles and articles requiring bent wood. Michigan was once the leading state in the production of ash lumber but we now supply less than 10 percent of the total national output.

A hardy tree, white ash is found throughout the state growing on a variety of soils in mixture with other hardwoods such as basswood, oak, hickory, soft maple and elm in the southern part of the state, and beech, yellow birch, sugar maple and hemlock in the north. It never forms a major part of a forest but occurs scattered or in small groups.

While trees over 100 feet high and five feet in diameter were not uncommon in the past, such specimens are rare today, and individuals two to three feet in diameter and 60 to 80 feet high are now considered large. In the forest, white ash has a narrow, pointed crown composed of slender lateral branches, coarse twigs, and a straight, clear, columnar trunk. When grown in the open, it is definitely a round-topped, low-branching tree. It is fast-growing and moderately tolerant. The root system is fibrous and deep, and vigorous sprouts grow from the stumps. Like the maples, the branching is opposite and each pair of small twigs is set at nearly right angles to the pairs above and below it.

The bark on the main trunk is ashy-gray and is distinctively marked by deep furrows and a network of firm, narrow, flattened ridges forming diamond-shaped or wedge-shaped fissures. On the new growth, the bark is smooth, dark green in color, becoming light brown or gray, often covered with a waxy bloom.

Arranged oppositely on the stems, the leaves are compound, eight to 12 inches long, with usually seven oval, pointed, round-based leaflets, each three to five inches long and one to two inches wide. The leaflets are short-stalked with smooth or slightly toothed margins. Thin and firm, they are bright green above and paler beneath. The main leaf stem is stiff and grooved. The opposite arrangement of the leaves distinguishes the ash from the hickories and walnuts whose compound leaves are arranged alternately. The short-stalked leaflets of the white ash will distinguish this species from the black ash whose leaflets have no stalks.

Before the late appearing leaves develop, the flowers form, usually in May, with staminate and pistillate on separate trees. They are arranged in loose clusters or panicles on shoots of the preceding year. In August and September, the seeds ripen, often persisting on the tree in drooping bunches until mid-winter or the following spring. The seeds are single, at the stem end of a tapered, round-tipped, paddle-shaped wing which is one to two inches long and ¼-inch wide. The seed kernel is thick and only partially surrounded by the wing. Approximately 6,000 seeds will weigh a pound.

The terminal winter bud is short, rounded and rusty or dark brown in color. The lateral buds are smaller, the first pair settled close beside the terminal one. In black ash the first pair of lateral buds is considerably below the terminal bud.

While relatively free from serious diseases, the white ash has many insects which may damage or destroy it. Small trees are often infested and occasionally killed by the oystershell scale. The carpenter worm often ruins commercial timber by tunnneling into the heartwood. The fall cankerworm may cause damage by defoliation. The sapwood of seasoned ash is often completely pulverized by powderpost beetles which may leave only a thin exterior shell of wood.

White ash wood is heavy (42 pounds per cubic foot when dry), strong, hard, tough, elastic and shock resisting. The light brown heartwood and thick lighter-colored sapwood are sharply divided. Its grain is straight and rather coarse, wearing smooth with use. These properties attach to white ash a long list of useful products. Its shock-resisting and bending abilities fit it for use in ball bats, tennis racquets, snowshoes, skis, polo and hockey sticks, oars and paddles, long tool handles and barrels. Its toughness makes it useful for agricultural implements, rollers, shuttles, bobbins and looms, and the fact that it imparts no odor or taste makes it the best wood for butter tubs. Its primary faults are that it nails poorly and is not durable in continually moist locations. Much of the white ash timber cut in southern Michigan is shipped in round form to mills in Ohio and Indiana for manufacture into tool handles.

Identifying characteristics: Leaves opposite, compound, with usually seven short-stalked, smooth or slightly-toothed leaflets; seed kernel thick, partly surrounded by long, tapered, paddle-shaped wing. Terminal winter bud short, round, brown; lateral buds smaller, first pair at sides of terminal bud; bark ashy-gray, with diamond-shaped or wedge-shaped fissures.

BLACK ASH

Fraxinus nigra Marsh.

OF THE SIX SPECIES OF ASH ATTAINING commercial size in the United States, five are found east of the Rocky Mountains, and one on the West coast. Only three of the eastern ashes are important as log and lumber producers. These are white ash, green ash, and black ash, all of which are found in Michigan with only the white and black occurring in commercial quantities. The ashes are members of the olive family and are thus related to the lilacs and privets.

Black ash, also known as hoop, basket or swamp ash, is common throughout Michigan but attains its best size and form in the cold, northern swamps and river beds which are flooded part of the year. It is a slow-growing tree producing narrow, easily separated, annual growth layers of wood, a fact made use of by the Indians who pounded the fresh green wood until it separated along the annual growth rings, then cut the thin pieces into strips and used them in basket weaving. This practice is still used in many places in the state by Indian basket makers.

Occurring now and then in small, nearly pure patches, black ash is more often found as scattered trees in mixture with cedar, balsam fir, red maple, elm and balm-of-Gilead, and is typical of northern Michigan. It does not stand dense shading or crowding. In the forest it may grow to a height of 60 to 70 or more feet and 12 to 18 inches in diameter but is more often much smaller. Its branches are slender and upright, forming a narrow, open crown. The twigs are very coarse, stout and not numerous. The root system is shallow and fibrous. Neither graceful nor easily transplanted, it has little to recommend it as a landscape tree.

The bark on the small twigs is dark green turning to buff or ash-gray on the larger twigs, becoming dark gray and warty on the branches. The trunks are ash-gray, very shallowly fissured, the ridges scaly or corky, often soft and mealy, flaking off when rubbed. Black ash bark does not have the diamond-shaped fissuring characteristic of white ash.

The leaves are opposite, compound, 12 to 16 inches long, composed of seven to 11 opposite leaflets, each three to five inches long and one to two inches wide. With the exception of the terminal one, the leaflets are not stalked as in white ash but are "sessile," growing directly from the leaf stem. They are thin and firm, taper-pointed at the tips, rounded or wedge-shaped at the base with small, blunt teeth around the margin. Dark, shiny green above, they are paler beneath with fine hairs where the leaflets and stems join. The leaf stem is stout and grooved.

Flowers are produced in May before the leaves, some staminate, some pistillate, and some perfact (i.e., both stamens and pistils in the same flower), each kind found on separate trees or all on the same tree. They occur in loose clusters or panicles on the preceding year's shoots. The fruit matures in August and September in long drooping clusters, falling at that time or remaining on the tree until winter or spring. Whereas white ash seed kernels are rounded and only partly surrounded by the wing, those of black ash are flattened and nearly completely surrounded by the wing. The wings are 1½-inches long and ¼- to ½-inch wide, blunt or often notched at the end. The number of seeds per pound is approximately 3,000.

The terminal winter buds are more pointed than in white ash and are nearly black in color. The first pair of lateral buds is some distance below the terminal bud, whereas in white ash the first pair of lateral buds is close to the terminal bud, in fact almost touching it.

Like white ash, the black ash is comparatively free from serious diseases. The oystershell scale often infests it in the southern part of the state and various defoliators may attack it, but its occurrence as a scattered tree in mixture with other species does not favor serious insect infestations.

Commercially, black ash lumber is usually sold with white ash under the name "ash." However, in some trade channels, particularly in the South, it is separated from white ash and sold as brown ash or "pumpkin ash." Most of the black ash is cut in the Upper Peninsula.

Considerably lighter in weight than white ash, black ash weighs 36 pounds per cubic foot, air-dry. It is tough, coarse-grained, rather soft, with thin, light-colored sapwood, and ranks below white ash in strength. Its uses are not as extensive as those of white ash since it will not stand as much hard wear or pounding. Principal uses include vehicle stock, furniture, ties, baskets, chair bottoms, hoops, butter tubs and some athletic equipment. Because of its dark color and pleasing figure, it is occasionally used in cabinet work and interior finishing.

Identifying characteristics: Leaves opposite, compound, with seven to 11 finely-toothed, sessile leaflets; seed kernels flat, nearly completely surrounded by broad, often notched wing; terminal winter bud pointed, black; lateral buds smaller, first pair some distance below the terminal; bark ash-gray, corky or mealy, flaking off when rubbed; found in cold, wet soils.

BLACK GUM

Nyssa sylvatica Marsh.

BLACK GUM IS ONE OF SOUTHERN MICHigan's least common trees, and because of its fondness for dense forests and swampy soils, it is not often observed. To anyone familiar with the dogwoods, however, this species should not be difficult to identify for it is a member of the same family and its leaves have the same characteristics.

One of four species of the genus *Nyssa*, black gum is the only one found in Michigan. All are water-loving, but black gum less so than the others. The watery haunts and the graceful beauty of these trees are appropriately referred to in the botanical name, for Nyssa was a water nymph in Greek mythology. The Indians called this species "tupelo," a name by which it is still generally known today; and in many localities it is also referred to as "sour gum" or "pepperidge."

Like many of the trees in the great central hardwood region of the eastern United States, black gum reaches the northern limits of its range in the south half of the Lower Peninsula of Michigan, extending as far north as Bay County on the eastern side and Manistee County on the west side. Outside of Michigan it extends east to the Atlantic Coast and south to the Gulf of Mexico. Inhabiting forested swamp borders and low wet lands, it is associated with red and silver maples, swamp oaks, black ash, basswood, and sycamore.

Black gum is ordinarily a comparatively small tree, becoming at maturity only 50 to 60 feet in height with trunks one to two feet in diameter. Maximum sizes attained are 125 feet tall and five feet in diameter. The continuous, often crooked, trunk extends into a broadly-rounded or flat-topped crown composed of slender, spreading, horizontal or drooping, angular branches and ascending branchlets supporting flattened leaf sprays. The root system is shallow and spreading.

Black gum buds are ¼- to ⅛-inch long, egg-shaped, and dark red. The twigs are greenish to light brown or orange in color, smooth or slightly downy, with visible pale lenticels. The pith in the twigs is divided by thin partitions. The bark on old trunks is dark reddish brown to gray, thick and rough. The surface may be broken into long, coarse, vertical ridges with deep furrows, or it may be made up of small, irregular plates broken by a network of shallow furrows giving it an "alligator hide" appearance. Both types of bark are often present on the same trunk.

The leaves of black gum are alternate, two to five inches long and approximately one-half as wide with the widest part at or just above the middle. They are smooth margined, oval in general outline, tapering to both ends, with a blunt tip and short petiole. Thick and somewhat leathery in texture, they are shiny dark green on the upper surface and pale, often slightly hairy, below. The distinct veins are parallel, wide-spaced, and curve in slightly toward the tip of the leaf. Black gum is one of the first trees to change color in the fall, and is known for the brilliant and variable hues of its autumn foliage. The upper surface of the leaves turns to shades varying from brick-red to scarlet, maroon or purple. Often only part of the leaf changes color, the rest remaining bright green.

In May and June with the developing leaves the inconspicuous greenish flowers appear, supported by slender, downy stems. Sometimes perfect and sometimes uni-sexual, the two flower forms occur on different trees. The small, fleshy fruits mature in September and October. They are oval shaped, approximately ½-inch long, blue-black in color, with sour flesh and a ribbed pit. They are a favorite food of many birds. There are an average of 3,300 cleaned seeds per pound.

Perhaps the worst enemies of the black gum are the heart rots which decay the center of the stems, often at an early age, producing hollow trees. Such decays are the cause of frequent breakage in the tops of the trees. Hollow sections of the trunk were at one time used for beehives.

As a landscape tree black gum has much to recommend it. It possesses a distinctive form which is picturesque in both summer and winter, and its early fall coloring is unexcelled. In spite of the fact that wild trees are very difficult to transplant, nursery-grown trees should do well if planted in a moist, somewhat protected site.

The wood of black gum is soft and only moderately heavy, weighing approximately 35 pounds per cubic foot in an air-dry condition. Its interwoven fibers, however, make it strong and extremely tough. The sapwood is thick and light colored, while the heartwood is dark, varying from yellow to reddish brown, often streaked with lighter or darker patches. The lumber warps easily and has a high percentage of shrinkage; and although black gum grows on wet sites, its wood is not durable in contact with the soil.

Once considered worthless, this species now has many uses most of which depend upon its toughness. These uses include such items as chopping bowls, hatters' blocks, scaffolding, furniture core stock, and handles for heavy tools. In the form of veneer, it is used extensively in agricultural containers and for large shipping crates for machinery and appliances. Its dark color shows light paints or chalk well and it can easily be marked for shipment.

Identifying characteristics: Leaves alternate, smooth margined, tapering to both ends; veins parallel, wide spaced, curving slightly toward tip; leaf sprays flattened; branchlets ascending; old bark with coarse vertical ridges or small irregular plates, both kinds often on same trunk; fruit ½-inch long, blue-black, fleshy, sour.

GINKGO

Ginkgo biloba L.

THE EXOTIC GINKGO, OR MAIDENHAIR tree, is not a common tree in Michigan, but it is interesting enough and exists often enough as planted specimens to make it worthy of inclusion among trees worth knowing. "Ginkgo" (pronounced with a hard or soft "g") is the Chinese name for this tree, and refers to the silvery white, edible seeds. The name "maidenhair tree" is a reference to the unique fan-shaped leaves which resemble the fronds of the maidenhair fern.

Gingko is of interest, not only because of its charm and usefulness in urban parks and along city streets, but because of its unique place in the universe of plants. It is the only living survivor of a family of fossilized plants, intermediate between ferns and conifers, which flourished millions of years ago during the Age of Reptiles, the Carboniferous period of geological history. Fossil leaves, identical to those growing today, have been found in many parts of the world, from the Arctic region to the south temperate zone, indicating that ginkgo was once widespread.

The living descendants of ginkgo were cultivated for untold centuries in Chinese temple gardens; and it was introduced into Japan perhaps a thousand years ago judging from the age of living specimins in gardens there. Until early in this century, these Oriental gardens were believed to harbor the only survivors of this living fossil, and hence were considered to be responsible for its preservation since it had not been known to exist anywhere in the wild. However, isolated, "spontaneous" groves are now known to exist in mountainous areas near the Yangtze River in eastern China. The temple gardens, nevertheless, served as the source for the wide dissemination of this unusual tree in Asia and Europe, and later in America, where it was introduced in 1784. One of these original plantings is reported to be alive and well in Fairmount Park in Philadelphia.

In the two centuries since its introduction, ginkgo has been planted as an ornamental throughout northeastern United States and in Pacific coast areas. In Michigan it is found mostly in the southern half of the Lower Peninsula; but it is nowhere common, a fact which makes it all the more interesting when it is discovered. It has a pleasing, symmetrical form, broadly spire-like when young, with branches angling upward from the stem at about a 45 degree angle. It is long-lived, with old individuals developing broad, open crowns, forming pleasant shade trees. Slow-growing when young, it ultimately attains heights of 60 to 80 feet or more with a straight trunk which may be two to four feet in diameter. Trees 100 feet tall and six feet in diameter are reported in Oriental temple gardens. It is easily propagated from

seed, is easy to transplant, and has no serious diseases or insect pests.

Because of its ability to thrive on a variety of soils, and particularly for its tolerance of smoke, dust, and other adverse city conditions, ginkgo is ideal for planting in situations where these qualities are needed. Its principal drawback is found in the slippery, ill-smelling fruits produced by the female trees. This aspect is overcome by planting only the male trees.

The bark on the young twigs is red-brown to gray-brown and smooth. On old trunks it is ash-gray tinged with brown, and roughened by long, deep, vertical furrows. The winter buds are about ⅛ inch long, cone shaped, chestnut brown, and smooth.

The long-stemmed leaves occur alternately along the twigs, as well as in clusters of three to six on short spurs. They are uniquely fan-shaped, two to four inches wide with a deep notch in the center of the wavy, rounded edge, dividing the leaf into two lobes, hence the botanical name "*biloba.*" They are thin and firm, with fine parallel veins, and no mid-rib. Bright green in the summer, they turn to clear butter yellow in the fall.

The flowers appear in May along with the leaves, male and female on different trees. The yellow male or staminate flowers are in drooping catkins about 1 to 1½ inches long; the female or pistillate flowers are in pairs on erect stalks. Following pollination, fertilization is accomplished by free-swimming sperms, as in ferns, which emerge from a pollen tube within the developing seed. Normally only one seed of the flower pair develops. In the fall the plum-like fruits mature. They are about one inch in diameter, green to orange-yellow in color, and contain a soft pulp with the smell and taste of rancid butter (i.e., butyric acid). The seed is a silvery white, almond flavored nut. In China and Japan the nuts are considered a delicacy and are eaten roasted in soups, or baked with meat or fowl.

The wood is yellowish to red-brown in color, with thin, lighter colored sapwood. It is soft, weak and light in weight, and has no commercial use.

———

Identifying characteristics: Leaves alternate, mostly clustered on spurs, fan-shaped, no mid-rib, with notched edge forming two lobes; male and female trees separate; fruit plum-like, ill-smelling; bark brown-gray, with deep, vertical furrows.

83

AILANTHUS

Ailanthus altissima (Mill.) Swingle

Although not an American tree, ailanthus or tree-of-heaven has become so naturalized and widespread in the United States and in Michigan as to be considered almost a part of the native flora. The history of its introduction into this country goes back to England where it had been brought from its native China in about 1750 with the hope that it would provide food for silkworms there as it did in China. The enterprise failed, but the tree became popular for its rapid growth and interesting foliage.

Ailanthus was brought to America in 1784, and in the early 1800's was widely disseminated to large cities as an ornamental tree and because of its presumed ability to absorb malarial poisons from the atmosphere. However, several severe outbreaks of malaria dispelled this myth, and the tree was then blamed for giving off the poisons which it had absorbed. This, together with infestations of worms on the leaves brought about efforts to eradicate it.

The great height to which ailanthus grows in China, where it reaches 100 feet or more, is said to give rise to the name "tree-of-heaven." Its critics, however, are more inclined to refer to it as "stinktree," or "stinkweed," or by other equally uncomplimentary names, for its leaves, when bruised, and its staminate flowers give off a disagreeable odor. Also, its propensity for taking root in waste places where no other trees will grow has given it a weed-tree role in the minds of many. This is the tree which comes up through the cracks in sidewalks and pavements, in railroad freight yards, and at the foundations of abondoned buildings, the environment characterized in the book, "A Tree Grows in Brooklyn." That tree was an ailanthus.

In the right places this much maligned "weed" becomes an attractive and graceful tree with an oriental bearing. Where maintenance is a problem and conditions are severe, such as one might find in an urban schoolyard or playground, this "roughneck" can be the answer to the need for beauty and shade.

Through years of plantings for ornamental purposes, for "quick shade," and for shelterbelts, the range of ailanthus has been extended from the East to the Pacific Coast. Locally it spreads by seeding and root suckering. In Michigan it is found principally in the southern part of the Lower Peninsula, though it occurs farther north. It is a rapid growing, short lived tree, in this region attaining heights of 40 to 60 feet or more, and diameters of one to two feet. Root sprouts may grow 6 to 10 feet in one season. Crowns are loose and spreading, with brittle branches and thick twigs. It will grow in almost any kind of soil, but young seedlings may win-

ter-kill. On home grounds its aggressive, penetrating roots may cause trouble with drains. While no longer recommended for planting as a landscape tree, its pleasing, irregular form, large plume-like leaves, and colorful seed clusters, together with its ability to withstand heat, drought and adverse city conditions, are much in its favor.

With the exception of the twigs, which are yellow to reddish brown, and velvety, the bark is a mottled steel gray, tight, and broken by shallow fissures exposing thin, lighter strips. The twigs exhibit a large yellow pith in cross-section.

The large, coarse leaves are alternate, pinnately compound and up to three feet in length, the largest of our tree leaves. They are composed of 11 to 41 lance-shaped, dark green leaflets, two to six inches long, with smooth margins except for two or more gland-tipped teeth near the base. The central leaf petiole, or rachis, is swollen at the base, enlarging into a grooved hoof-like or heart shaped end where it attaches to the twig. In autumn the leaves have the unusual characteristic of dropping their leaflets before the petioles fall.

In June after the leaves have formed, the yellowish green flowers appear in upright clusters 6 to 12 inches long, male and female flowers on different trees. It is the male or staminate flowers which are ill-smelling, and hence only the female trees should be planted or encouraged. The showy, large, hanging clusters of spirally twisted, winged seeds develop during the summer, changing through phases of pale green, pink, orange, red, bronze or yellow before turning to a dry brown at maturity. These colorful stages make interesting bouquets. The single seed forms a conspicuous "eye" in the center of each elongated wing. The winter buds are about ⅛ inch long, brown and woolly, set in the notch of the large leaf scar.

The wood of ailanthus is of no commercial value, although it is claimed that its satiny appearance makes it an interesting cabinet wood. Physically it is soft and weak with a coarse open grain. The heartwood is pale yellow-brown in color; the sapwood is lighter colored and thick.

———

Identifying characteristics: Leaves alternate, compound, may be three feet long, with numerous smooth-margined leaflets; male and female flowers on different trees; the staminate ill-smelling; seeds winged, in large colorful clusters; twigs with thick yellow pith; bark steel gray, minutely fissured.

NORTHERN CATALPA

Catalpa speciosa Warder

THE NORTHERN OR HARDY CATALPA IS not native to Michigan, although it is common in the state, particularly in the Lower Peninsula where it has been planted as a lawn and landscape tree because of its interesting form and showy flowers. Its fast growth and tolerance of such harsh city conditions as smoke, drought and poor soil make it valuable in urban areas, and its general hardiness has made it useful in shelterbelt plantings in the Great Plains. Because of its durable wood, it is occasionally set out in small plantations to be cut for fence posts.

Of the seven or more species of the genus *Catalpa* found throughout the world, two are native to the United States — the southern catalpa, a small tree found in the Gulf States, and the larger northern catalpa, whose natural range is limited to a small area in the central Mississippi Valley. However, northern catalpa has become naturalized through planting over a much wider area including most of the eastern United States and the Pacific Northwest. In its native range it occurs scattered in forests growing on rich bottomland soils. Other names by which the catalpas are known locally are catawba, cigar tree, and Indian bean.

As normally seen in Michigan, catalpa is an open-grown, irregular, round-topped tree with a short trunk and wide-spreading, low hanging, crooked branches and stiff, coarse branchlets. It usually attains heights of 40 to 60 feet with trunks two to three feet in diameter. Under ideal growing conditions, maximum sizes of 120 feet in height and four and one-half feet in diameter may be reached. Growth is rapid and trunks may add an inch in diameter annually when young; but the trees are relatively short-lived, 40 years being considered old. Catalpa is easily propagated by seeds, cuttings or layering, and is easy to transplant. Although its landscape and street tree values have diminished in recent years in favor of smaller trees, it is, none-the-less, still planted for these purposes.

The bark on the young twigs is green to brown, often with a whitish bloom and dotted with light colored lenticels. On the older branches and trunks it is reddish-brown to gray-brown and broken into thick scales or vertical ridges. The twigs contain a soft, white pith.

Catalpa leaves are among the largest tree leaves found in Michigan, being 8 to 12 inches long and 6 to 8 inches wide. They are heart-shaped, smooth margined, and long stemmed, occurring in whorls of three, or occasionally in opposite pairs. There is a small nectar gland at the base of each leaf stem. They are thick and firm, dark green on the upper surface, pale green and somewhat downy beneath. They are easily affected by frosts, and are among the first leaves to drop in the fall. The scars left on the twigs by the leaf stems are large, oval and depressed with a characteristic inner circle of smaller scars. The winter buds are inconspicuous, almost hidden on the upper rim of the leaf scars.

In June after the leaves are full grown, the showy flowers develop in open, branched, pyramidal clusters six to seven inches high. The bell-shaped flowers are approximately two inches long, five lobed, and white with yellow streaks and purple dots in the throat. They contain a very sweet nectar.

The long, narrow, cylindrical seed pods or "cigars" form in early autumn and hang on the trees throughout the winter, opening and dispersing their seeds in the spring. The pods are 10 to 20 inches long and one-half inch in diameter, green at first, then brown. The seeds are small papery flakes, about one inch long with tufts of hairs on each end. A pound of seeds will number about 23,000.

Catalpa has few serious pests although it is easily injured by frosts, and high winds may break the brittle branches. The larvae of a moth known as the catalpa sphinx may cause defoliation but to fishermen such attacks may be welcome since this worm is considered to be excellent bait. Certain midges and leaf miners, as well as leaf-spotting diseases, may be troublesome, but seldom cause more than temporary injury.

The wood of catalpa is light brown to olive brown in color, soft, straight grained, with rather coarse texture. It has an unpleasant odor when freshly cut. It is light in weight, a cubic foot of seasoned wood weighing only approximately 26 pounds. It is easy to work and holds its shape well, but its uses are limited as is also the supply. The durability of the heartwood in contact with the soil makes it valuable for fence posts. Other uses include picture frames, interior finish and furniture frames.

Identifying characteristics: Leaves opposite or whorled, 8 to 12 inches long and 6 to 8 inches wide, heart-shaped, margins smooth; flowers white, showy, two inches long; seeds in slender pods 10 to 20 inches long, persistent through winter; leaf scars prominent; winter buds inconspicuous.

85

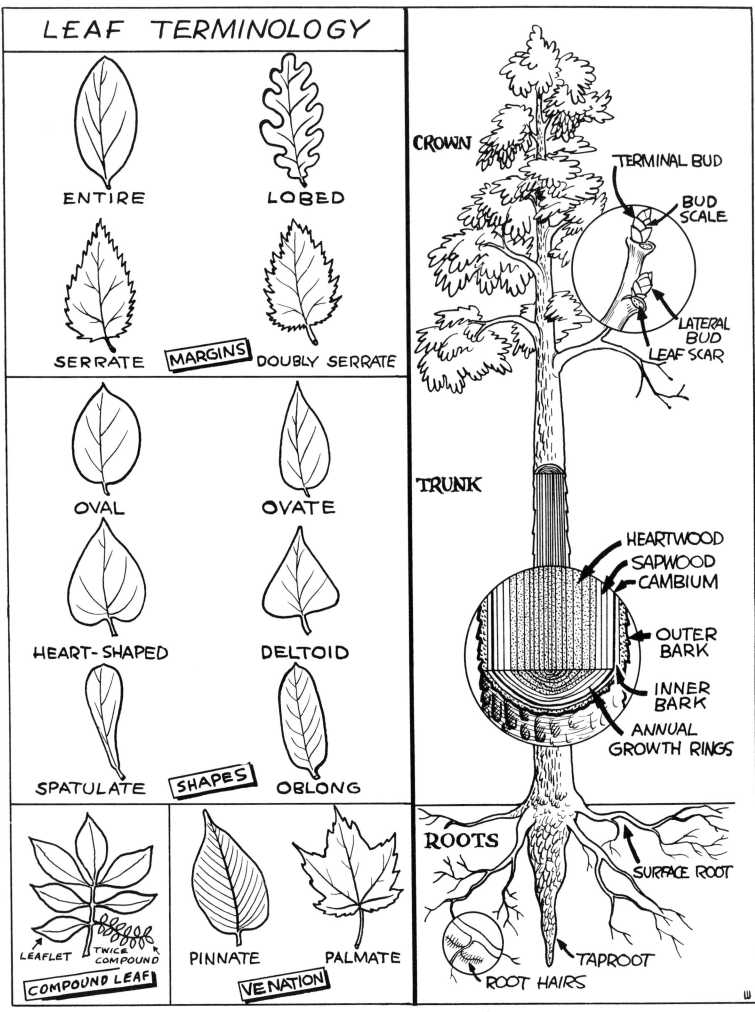

LEAF TERMINOLOGY

ENTIRE

LOBED

SERRATE

MARGINS

DOUBLY SERRATE

OVAL

OVATE

HEART-SHAPED

DELTOID

SPATULATE

SHAPES

OBLONG

LEAFLET **TWICE COMPOUND**

COMPOUND LEAF

PINNATE

PALMATE

VENATION

CROWN

TERMINAL BUD

BUD SCALE

LATERAL BUD

LEAF SCAR

TRUNK

HEARTWOOD

SAPWOOD

CAMBIUM

OUTER BARK

INNER BARK

ANNUAL GROWTH RINGS

ROOTS

SURFACE ROOT

TAPROOT

ROOT HAIRS

GLOSSARY

Annual ring—A narrow band usually visible in wood cross-section marking a year's growth.

Air-dry—A standard term used to denote 12 percent moisture content in wood or lumber.

Board foot—A unit of measure for lumber or standing timber. A board measuring 12 inches square and 1 inch thick equals 1 board foot. (Abbrev.: bd. ft.).

Bole—The trunk of a tree.

Bract—A small leaflike appendage at the base of a flower or flower cluster.

Bud scale—Modified leaves covering a bud.

Calyx—The basal cup of a flower, composed of small leaflike scales, usually green.

Catkin—A flexible, usually drooping stem bearing either male or female flowers.

Compound leaf—A leaf made up of several separate leaflets attached to a common leaf stem.

Cone—A fruit with woody, overlapping scales.

Conifer—A tree which produces its seeds in cones.

Coniferous—A term applied to that group of trees which produces its seeds in cones.

Cord—A unit of measure for stacked wood. A standard cord measures 4 ft. x 4 ft. x 8 ft. and contains 128 cubic feet (actually about 90 cubic feet of solid wood). A stove cord or firewood cord measures 16 in. x 4 ft. x 8 ft., one third of a standard cord.

Cubic foot—A unit of measure 12 inches square and 12 inches thick. In forestry this unit is frequently used to express total volume of wood in timber stands.

Cull—A term applied to trees or forest products rejected because of defects.

Deciduous—A term applied to those trees which lose their leaves annually, usually at the end of the growing season.

Dozy—Referring to rot in timber or lumber. Usually a soft, punky decay which weakens the wood.

Family—A group of genera related in certain broad characteristics; as for example, the needle-bearing trees (pine, spruce, fir, etc.) which all belong to the family, *Pinaceae*.

Forest type—A descriptive term used to group stands of similar character as regards composition and development by which they can be differentiated from other groups of stands.

Forestry—The scientific management of forests and forest land for the continuous production of goods and services.

Genus—A subdivision of a family composed of closely related species, such as the oaks, genus: *Quercus*.

Glabrous—Smooth, without hairs.

Hardwood—In general the broadleaved trees are classed as hardwoods. The term also applies to the lumber produced from these trees even though it may be fairly soft.

Heartwood—The central core of a woody stem or trunk which gives it strength. It is composed of dead cells, and is often distinguished from the sapwood by its darker color.

Intolerant—Pertaining to those trees which cannot develop and grow in the shade of or in close competition with other trees.

Leaf scar—The scar left on the twig where a leaf was attached. Leaf scars vary in size and shape with different species and are frequently useful in winter identification of hardwoods.

Leaflet—One of the several separate divisions of a compound leaf.

Lenticel—A corky growth on young or sometimes older bark, which admits air to the interior of the twig or branch.

Merchantable Timber—Trees of sufficient size and quality to yield wood products which can be profitably marketed.

Mid-rib—The central vein or main rib of a leaf.

Naturalized—Of foreign origin, but established and reproducing itself as if native.

Ovulate—Referring to those flowers, as in the conifers, which possess ovules, and which produce seeds after fertilization.

Panicle—A floral arrangement consisting of a central stalk supporting several flowers on short, branched stalks.

Perfect—Referring to those flowers which contain both stamens and pistils.

Petiole—The stalk of a leaf.

Pioneer species—A tree species which first comes into a clearing. Usually short-lived, and not the ultimate species which will occupy the site.

Pistillate—Referring to those flowers which possess only pistils, the female seed-producing organs.

Poletimber—Small trees, (between approximately 5 and 10 inches in diameter) large enough for posts and pulpwood, but usually too small to be sawed into lumber. With most species poletimber becomes sawtimber if left to grow.

Pulpwood—Wood cut primarily for manufacture into pulp or chips for paper and various pressed board products.

Samara—A dry, single-seeded, winged fruit.

Sapwood—The living, usually light-colored, band of wood surrounding the heartwood, through which sap flows from the roots to the leaves.

Saw log—A log large enough to be sawed into lumber and other products of a sawmill. In eastern U. S. saw logs are generally 10 inches or more in diameter and 8 to 16 feet long.

Sawtimber—Trees large enough to yield logs suitable for sawing into lumber and other products.

Serrate—Toothed with fine, sharp teeth.

Sessile—Leaflets which do not have stalks or stems but which are attached directly by the base are said to be sessile.

Silviculture—The art of producing and tending a forest.

Simple—A single leaf, not compound.

Site—An area considered with reference to its capacity to produce forests or other vegetation; the combination of biotic, climatic, and soil conditions of an area.

Softwood—In general the coniferous trees are classed as softwoods. The term also applies to lumber produced from these trees.

Species—Generally the final subdivision in plant or animal classification, composed of individuals exhibiting identical or nearly identical biological characteristics, as: white oak, *Quercus alba*.

Spike—A floral arrangement consisting of a central stalk supporting several stemless flowers.

Staminate—Referring to those flowers which possess only stamens, the male pollen-producing organs.

Tolerant—Pertaining to those trees which can endure shading and the close competition of other trees.

Unisexual—Referring to flowers which have either stamens or pistils but not both; i.e., not perfect.

Veneer—A thin sheet of wood peeled, sliced or sawed from a log.

Whorl—A spoke-like arrangement of leaves or branches around a stem.

WOOD TO BURN

Fireplaces and wood-burning stoves make use of a renewable fuel resource, one that is presently in plentiful supply, and generally available at reasonable prices, cut and delivered. In some localities it is obtainable as residue from mills, or in tree form from public forest lands under cutting permit. While woodstoves are much more efficient than fireplaces as serious sources of heat, the glowing hearth offers a pleasing focal point in a room, and provides warmth to both body and spirit.

Choosing the kinds of wood to burn in the fireplace should be a selective process, since each wood species can offer something different in heat value or aroma. Softwoods like pine, spruce, and fir, are easy to ignite because they are resinous. They burn briskly with a hot flame. However, since a fire built entirely of softwoods burns out quickly, it requires frequent attention and replenishment. Resinous woods and the soft hardwoods like aspen and basswood are best for a quick warming fire and for kindling.

For a long lasting, hotter fire it is best to use the heavier hardwoods such as hickory, oak, beech, maple and ash, which burns less vigorously than softwoods and with a shorter flame. Oak gives the most uniform and lowest flames, and produces steady, glowing coals. For an easily ignited and long-lasting fire hardwoods and softwoods should be mixed. Aroma is best derived from the woods of fruit trees such as apple and cherry, and nut trees such as beech and hickory.

Fuelwood is normally cut into approximately 16-inch lengths and sold as a "stove" cord or "firewood" cord, which is one-third of a standard cord (4x4x8 feet). Freshly cut "green" wood is difficult to burn. Split sections or round pieces should be stacked and allowed to "season" for six months to a year before using.

The heat that a fireplace or stove log produces depends on the concentration of woody material, resin, water, and ash. Since woods are of different compositions, they ignite at different temperatures and give off different intensities of heat. When wood is compared to fossil fuels, a full or standard cord of hickory is approximately equal in heating value to a ton of hard coal. The accompanying table shows the relative heat values of a variety of seasoned woods arranged in descending order from those with approximately 100 per cent cord-to-coal equivalent to the lowest with about 50 per cent equivalent.

FUELWOOD RANKED BY PERCENT OF HEAT IN A STANDARD CORD COMPARED TO A TON OF COAL

(listed in descending order within classes)

VERY HIGH — 95 to 100%

Shagbark hickory	Ironwood
Dogwood	White oak
Black locust	Honeylocust
Swamp white oak	Bitternut hickory

HIGH — 85 to 95%

Blue beech	Sugar maple
Bur oak	Red oak
Black oak	Yellow birch
Rock elm	Mulberry
Beech	Apple

MEDIUM — 70 to 85%

White birch	American elm
Walnut	Silver maple
Slippery elm	Ashes
Tamarack	Red pine
Black cherry	Red cedar
Hackberry	Sycamore
Red maple	

LOW — 50 to 70%

Jack pine	Balsam fir
Black spruce	Aspens
White spruce	White pine
Hemlock	Willow
Sassafras	Basswood
Tulip poplar	Balm-of Gilead
Cottonwood	White cedar